VIRTUOUS & VICTORIOUS

Embrace strength, grace and divine wisdom
through scripture, prayer and devotion.

30 DAY DEVOTIONAL FOR THE PROVERBS 31 WOMAN

VISIONARIES:
CHAUNDRA GORE &
DR. PAULETTE HARPER

Published by A Divine Collaboration
Lithia, FL 33547
© 2025 A Divine Collaboration

Book Cover Design: - Prophetess Chaundra Gore

Editing and Interior Book Design & Formatting: Dynamic Image Publications

All rights reserved. No part of this book may be used or reproduced, stored in or introduced into a retrieval system, or transmitted in any form including, photocopying, electronic or mechanical, recording or by any means without the express written consent from the author.

Scripture quotations marked "NKJV" are taken from the New King James Version. Copyright © 1982 by Thomas Nelson, Inc. Used by permission. All rights reserved.

Scripture quotations marked "KJV" are taken from the Holy Bible, King James Version, Cambridge, 1769. Used by permission.

Scriptures marked NIV are taken from the NEW INTERNATIONAL VERSION (NIV): Scripture taken from THE HOLY BIBLE, NEW INTERNATIONAL VERSION ®. Copyright© 1973, 1978, 1984, 2011 by Biblica, Inc.TM. Used by permission of Zondervan

Scripture quotations taken from the (NASB®) New American Standard Bible®, Copyright © 1960, 1971, 1977, 1995, 2020 by The Lockman Foundation. Used by permission. All rights reserved. http://www.lockman.org/

Scripture quotations are from The ESV® Bible (The Holy Bible, English Standard Version®), copyright © 2001 by Crossway, a publishing ministry of Good News Publishers. Used by permission. All rights reserved.

Scriptures marked TLB are taken from the THE LIVING BIBLE (TLB): Scripture taken from THE LIVING BIBLE copyright© 1971. Used by permission of Tyndale House Publishers, Inc., Carol Stream, Illinois 60188. All rights reserved.

The Holy Bible, Tree of Life Version (TLV)
© 2011, 2012, 2013, 2014 & 2015 by the Messianic Jewish Family Bible Society

Library of Congress Cataloging-in-Publication Data

Paperback: ISBN: 9798285102564

Published and printed in the United States of America.

Table of Contents

Dedication 1
Proverbs 31 Epilogue 2
Foreword 4
Introduction 6
Opening Prayer 9
Day 1- Dr. Theresa A. Moseley 11
Day 2- Dr. Renyetta Johnson 13
Day 3- LeAnn Cerise Hendrick 15
Day 4- Donna Yates, LDA 17
Day 5- Coach Stephanie Johnson, MBA, NLP 19
Day 6- Evangelist Krystal K. Ryan 21
Day 7- Melissa Duran, RN, BC-FMP 23
Day 8- Minister Regina Amos 25
Day 9- Coach Renita Crump 27
Day 10- Pastor Patricia Saulsbury 29
Day 11- Mother in Zion Judy A. Wyndham 31
Day 12- Dr. JoAnne Hayes 33
Day 13- Evangelist Laticia Cunningham 35
Day 14- Christina Aguilar 37
Day 15- Isabelle Nifalar Ramos 39
Day 16- Sonja Sells 41
Day 17- Cristina Alaniz 43
Day 18- Dr. Regina A. Turner, M.Th.,Ph.D 45
Day 19- Prophetess Margaret D. Kirk 47
Day 20- Patricia Parada 49
Day 21- Lashon Dorsey, FNP-BC, MSN-PH 51
Day 22- Dr. Jewel White Williams 53

Day 23- Anita McAllister 55
Day 24- KoJuvona Telfair-Singleton, RN 57
Day 25- Dr. Rhonda A. Bolden 59
Day 26- Elder Dawn D. Braithwaite 61
Day 27- Candice Bryant 63
Day 28- Dr. LaTonya K. Poole 65
Day 29- Pastor Sheila P. Ingram 67
Day 30- Dr. Prophetess Natasha Lawson 69
Bonus Days
Prophetess Rebecca D. Huggins 71
Minister Peshon Allen 73
Closing Prayer 75
Afterword 77
Author Biographies 79
Write with Us 115
Calling All Readers 116

Dedication

To the woman in pursuit of purpose,
To the mother who prays through sleepless nights,
To the wife who builds her house with wisdom,
To the sister who uplifts others while quietly battling her own storms,
To the visionary, the servant, the trailblazer, the intercessor—
This is for you.

This devotional is lovingly dedicated to every woman of God who dares to rise daily with strength, dignity, and unwavering faith.

We also dedicate this work to our Heavenly Father—our source, sustainer, and strength. Without His wisdom, guidance, and grace, this book would not be possible.

To every contributor—your obedience to God's call and the courage to pour your heart onto these pages has created a legacy that will encourage generations of Proverbs 31 women to come.

And finally, to A Divine Collaboration—thank you for answering the call to gather, equip, and empower women through the Word. Your leadership has ignited a movement of virtue and victory that will echo far beyond these 30 days.

With love, honor, and faith,
A Divine Collaboration Founders

Epilogue:
The Wife of Noble Character

10 [a] A wife of noble character who can find?
She is worth far more than rubies.
11 Her husband has full confidence in her
and lacks nothing of value.
12 She brings him good, not harm,
all the days of her life.
13 She selects wool and flax
and works with eager hands.
14 She is like the merchant ships,
bringing her food from afar.
15 She gets up while it is still night;
she provides food for her family
and portions for her female servants.
16 She considers a field and buys it;
out of her earnings she plants a vineyard.
17 She sets about her work vigorously;
her arms are strong for her tasks.
18 She sees that her trading is profitable,
and her lamp does not go out at night.
19 In her hand she holds the distaff
and grasps the spindle with her fingers.
20 She opens her arms to the poor
and extends her hands to the needy.
21 When it snows, she has no fear for her household;
for all of them are clothed in scarlet.
22 She makes coverings for her bed;
she is clothed in fine linen and purple.
23 Her husband is respected at the city gate,
where he takes his seat among the elders of the land.
24 She makes linen garments and sells them,
and supplies the merchants with sashes.

^{25}She is clothed with strength and dignity;
she can laugh at the days to come.
^{26}She speaks with wisdom,
and faithful instruction is on her tongue.
^{27}She watches over the affairs of her household
and does not eat the bread of idleness.
^{28}Her children arise and call her blessed;
her husband also, and he praises her:
^{29}"Many women do noble things,
but you surpass them all."
^{30}Charm is deceptive, and beauty is fleeting;
but a woman who fears the Lord is to be praised.
^{31}Honor her for all that her hands have done,
and let her works bring her praise at the city gate.

Foreword:
Virtuous & Victorious:
A 30-Day Devotional for the Proverbs 31 Woman

The Proverbs 31 woman is often seen as the epitome of strength, grace, and virtue. But she is also a woman who knows how to rise above life's challenges, standing firm in her faith and trusting God's plan. The reflections in this book are meant to remind you that no matter where you are in your journey—whether you're stepping into leadership, navigating challenges, or seeking clarity—you are supported, equipped, and empowered to fulfill your divine purpose.

It is with great honor and excitement that I endorse Virtuous & Victorious: A 30-Day Devotional for the Proverbs 31 Woman. This book is not just a devotional; it is a powerful tool for women who desire to step into their divine calling and walk in the fullness of God's purpose for their lives.

As one of the visionaries behind Virtuous & Victorious: A 30-Day Devotional for the Proverbs 31 Woman, I have witnessed firsthand the passion, dedication, and commitment of the 34 incredible women who contributed to this project. Each of these women have poured their heart, wisdom, and experience into these pages, creating a transformative resource designed to inspire, encourage, and empower you. The devotionals within these pages offer much more than just words—they offer insights, revelations, and tools that will help you live out the Proverbs 31 life with confidence and grace.

In a world where women often juggle the demands of leadership, family, work, and personal growth, this devotional provides the spiritual guidance and practical wisdom needed to navigate these challenges with strength.

As you move through each page, you'll be reminded that you are not only virtuous but also victorious. This devotional will guide you in embracing your divine identity, walking in wisdom, and leading with courage.

I wholeheartedly endorse Virtuous & Victorious as an essential resource for any woman who seeks to live boldly, walk confidently, and embrace the fullness of her God-given destiny. Through this book, you will discover the power within you to lead, grow, and thrive as the Proverbs 31 woman that you were created to be.

May you be inspired, strengthened, and equipped as you embark on this 30-day journey, and may you walk away with a deeper understanding of the divine purpose that is uniquely yours.

With faith and excitement,

Dr. Paulette Harper

Co-Founder of A Divine Collaboration: The Virtuous & Victorious Sisterhood

Introduction
Virtuous & Victorious:
A 30-Day Devotional for the Proverbs 31 Woman

Hey, sis, you are not just any woman—you are a woman of virtue, strength, and divine purpose. You are called to rise, to lead, to serve, and to walk boldly in the identity God has given you. Life may bring challenges, seasons of uncertainty, and moments that test your faith, but through it all, you are victorious. Not because of your own strength, but because of the One who strengthens you.

This devotional was created with you in mind—a woman who is navigating the complexities of life with grace and faith. The Proverbs 31 Woman is more than just a biblical figure; she is the embodiment of strength, wisdom, and grace that we, as modern women, can aspire to. But let's be real: it's not always easy to live up to those expectations. We can easily get bogged down by our roles as wives, mothers, leaders, or employees, forgetting the divine power that resides in us.

Virtuous & Victorious was birthed out of a desire to help you reconnect with your true identity in Christ, to remind you of the truth that you are capable, worthy, and equipped for every purpose God has set before you. In this 30-day journey, you'll find encouragement, scripture, and reflections that will empower you to overcome doubt, embrace your strengths, and boldly transform into the woman God has destined you to be. Each day, we will dive deeper into the qualities of the Proverbs 31 woman— strength, wisdom, compassion, and faith—so you can begin to see yourself the way God sees you: virtuous, victorious, and unstoppable.

This devotional was created not just to uplift you, but to help you unlock the fullness of your potential. So take this journey with me. Let's walk together as women who stand firm in the promises of God, understanding that with Him, we are truly more than conquerors.

Virtuous & Victorious: A 30-Day Devotional for the Proverbs 31 Woman is more than a collection of stories—it is a transformational journey designed to empower, equip, and encourage you to live as the woman God created you to be. Through scripture, prayer, and real-life application, this devotional speaks to the heart of the Proverbs 31 woman— her faith, her wisdom, her resilience, and her unwavering commitment to God's calling.

This book is a labor of love, created by a powerful group of faith-filled women who have each experienced their own victories. Every devotion is rich with wisdom, authenticity, and practical insight, encouraging you to fully embrace your divine purpose.

No matter where you are on your path—leading with intention, balancing the demands of work and family, or searching for guidance in the next chapter—remember, you are empowered, upheld, and never walking this journey alone.

Throughout this devotional, you will be challenged to:

- Cultivate a heart that seeks God first in all things.
- Lead with confidence and humility.
- Walk in grace, knowing that your worth is rooted in Christ.
- Stand firm in faith, even when the road ahead is uncertain.

- Embrace your victories—both big and small—as evidence of God's faithfulness.

This is your time to rise, to embrace the virtuous and victorious life God has for you. No more shrinking back, no more second-guessing your worth. You are equipped, you are chosen, and you are called for such a time as this.

As you embark on this 30-day journey, let your heart be open, your faith be strengthened, and your spirit be renewed. Let these words remind you daily of the power that resides within you—the power to live as a woman of virtue and a woman of victory.

I am her—Virtuous & Victorious.

Dr. Paulette Harper

Co-Founder A Divine Collaboration: The Virtuous & Victorious Sisterhood

Opening Prayer
Virtuous & Victorious:
A 30-Day Devotional for the Proverbs 31 Woman

Heavenly Father, Mighty and Sovereign One, I come before You with gratitude, lifting up this devotional as a prophetic vessel that will transform the lives of every woman who reads it. I decree and declare that this book is anointed, divinely inspired, and carries the weight of heaven's wisdom. Let every word be infused with Your power, piercing through darkness and awakening the spirit of each and every reader.

Father, I decree that this book is a spiritual birthing chamber where destinies are unlocked, identities are affirmed, and purpose is made clear. As these words go forth, let them be a sword in the hands of the righteous, cutting through confusion, fear, and limitations. I declare that as women engage with these pages, they will boldly arise, clothed with strength and dignity, walking as victorious daughters of the King!

I prophesy that this devotional will be a well of living water, refreshing the weary, restoring the broken, and reigniting the fire of passion for Your purpose. Let this book serve as an altar where women encounter Your presence, hear Your voice, and receive divine revelation. I declare that every woman who opens these pages be drawn into the cleft of the Rock where she will experience transformation and emerge radiant, fearless, and unshakable.

In the name of Jesus, I break every assignment of the enemy that would attempt to hinder, delay, or distort the impact of this book. No weapon formed against it shall prosper! I decree that it will go forth with divine acceleration, reaching the hands of those who need it most.

This book shall be a beacon of light in the darkness, a trumpet of victory, and a mantle of wisdom that will rest upon generations to come.

I call forth supernatural doors of influence to open for this book! May it be carried into homes, ministries, businesses, and nations. I declare that it will be a tool of kingdom advancement, equipping Proverbs 31 women to walk in dominion, grace, and divine authority.

Now, Lord, breathe upon these words with Your ruach, Your breath of life. Let them stir up the gifts within every woman, breaking the chains of limitation, releasing fresh oil and activating her to move in her ordained purpose. I decree that testimonies will arise from this devotional, miracles will break forth, and new mantles will be placed upon those who receive this message in faith.

Father, I seal this book under the blood of Jesus and commission it into the earth for such a time as this. May it fulfill its divine assignment, bringing glory to Your name and establishing the next generation of virtuous and victorious women.

In the matchless name of Jesus, I decree it to be so! Amen and Amen! It is written. It is declared. It is done!

Dr. Prophetess Natasha Lawson

Day 1

"She opens her mouth with wisdom, and the teaching of kindness is on her tongue."

Proverbs 31:26 ESV

A virtuous woman embodies strength, dignity, respect, and wisdom. Her energy is positive and her aura is peaceful. She raises her family with kindness and grace all while identifying the gifts her family has within their souls. A virtuous woman uses her platform to share her wisdom with the world. Not just funded knowledge, but conventional wisdom aligned with scriptures. She understands her assignment to apply knowledge in a way that honors our God and brings peace to the world.

As I reflect on this verse, I think about how wisdom is not just having knowledge, but also how we apply our wisdom in our interactions with others. Remember: it's not what you say, but how you say it. Our words can uplift or discourage someone. Be compassionate and have empathy for others. A virtuous woman in the workplace provides her team with individual consideration, inspirational motivation, and intellectual stimulation. She motivates her staff to perform beyond their expectations. She is a nurturer and speaks with confidence and purpose.

A virtuous woman understands the difference between the physical body and the energetic body and the purpose of each. She shares her knowledge on how the energetic body aligns our emotions, mood, health, aura, and energetic toxins. When energy is stuck, it is difficult to be happy, peaceful, successful, or fulfilled. Being around negative energy can block the blessings that our God has for you.

Let God shape your thoughts and actions. When there is negative energy shield yourself through prayer, be intentional on how you speak to others.

Jeremiah 29:11 states: "For I know the plans I have for you, declares the Lord, plans to prosper you and not to harm you, plans to give you hope and a future." This verse is reassurance from God that there is a plan for each of us. When a virtuous woman shares this wisdom with her family, friends, coworkers, and anyone else, it provides a sense of hope and faith that all things are possible if you have faith and believe in the word. Wisdom is having the insight to apply knowledge while encompassing discernment, compassion, and empathy. A virtuous woman has wisdom, kindness, and leads with grace.

Prayer

Dear Heavenly Father, I thank You for the gift of wisdom. Continue to guide me on the right path to share my wisdom with the world. Show me the way to speak life unto those that are not living in their purpose and have not discovered their gifts. Show me the way to reach the masses that need love, hope, and peace. I pray that everyone learns how to use their gifts to live in their purpose and share their wisdom with the world. For I know we are all here to learn, to love, and to prosper. I pray these things in the name of Your son, Jesus Christ – Amen.

Dr. Theresa A. Moseley

Day 2

"She had a sister called Mary, who sat at the Lord's feet listening to what He said."
Luke 10:39 NIV

Have you ever noticed the still waters of a lake or the beauty that is reflected by all that is around it? There's a beautiful stillness in the image of Mary sitting at Jesus' feet. While Martha was busy with preparations, Mary made a different choice. She chose to be with Jesus, to listen, to learn, and to love Him with her attention. In a world that constantly pulls us toward busyness, Jesus still calls us to sit at His feet, to be discipled by Him, and to align our lives with His purposes.

Intimacy with the Father

Jesus modeled what an intimate relationship with the Father looks like. He often withdrew to quiet places to pray (Luke 5:16). He spoke what the Father told Him to speak (John 12:49). His life was in complete alignment with the will of God. If Jesus, being fully God and fully man, needed to be close to the Father, how much more do we?

When we prioritize intimacy with God, we begin to recognize His voice more clearly. We no longer live by the expectations of others or the demands of our schedules; we live by His leading.

Many of us want to be used by God in powerful ways, but the greatest calling we have isn't to do something for Him—it's to be with Him. Our effectiveness in the Kingdom starts with our intimacy with the King. When we are in an intimate relationship with God, knowing when to position ourselves as Mary and when to move like Martha becomes clearer.

Alignment with God's Plans

So many of us wrestle with questions like, What is my purpose? What am I called to do? The answer is found at Jesus' feet. When we spend time with Him, He aligns our desires with His. Proverbs 3:5-6 reminds us to trust in the Lord with all our hearts and lean not on our own understanding; in all our ways submit to Him, and He will make our paths straight.

Our job isn't to figure out every step ahead—it's to stay close to the One who directs our steps. He is faithful to lead us into His perfect will when we make Him our first priority.

When we sit at His feet, we absorb His wisdom, we learn His ways, and our hearts become more like His.

Sitting at the Feet of Jesus: A Call to Sit, Listen, and Follow

Today, Jesus is inviting you to slow down, to step away from distractions, and to sit at His feet. He wants to teach you, to speak to your heart, and to shape you into the person He created you to be. Will you accept His invitation?

Prayer

Jesus, I want to be near You. Teach me to sit at Your feet, to listen, and to learn from You. Align my heart with Yours and lead me in the plans You have for my life. Let my greatest pursuit always be You. Amen.

Dr. Renyetta Johnson

Day 3

"Strength and honour are her clothing; and she shall rejoice in time to come."
Proverbs 31:25 KJV

As far back as I can remember, I was surrounded by women who prayed, took care of the house and their families. All of these women (even the widows) possessed virtue. My mother taught me how to care for family and the home, manage finances, prepare healthy meals, carry myself appropriately both in and out of the home, but more importantly she taught me the importance of praying and believing in God.

I thought in order to be a virtuous woman I was expected to be perfect because of the examples I had growing up. As a young mother raising five children I found myself yearning for virtue. I cried out to God asking Him to show me the way, and He definitely did. My lack of understanding mixed with my desire to know and understand virtue allowed God to work in me and educate me through prayer and His word on what a virtuous woman really is.

After much studying and communication with the Lord, I soon learned that a virtuous woman was a unique woman, and that I was indeed a unique woman in God's eyes. God reassured me that even though I wasn't perfect, I still had characteristics that would set me apart from just an ordinary woman. The characteristics that defined me as a Proverbs 31 woman were already instilled in me. Some of those characteristics include dignity, patience, diligence, and generosity. God also showed me through trials and tribulations that I am a warrior. I am very strategic like my mother, and when troubles come I am equipped because I know how to battle in the spirit, through prayer with the Lord. It is a beautiful thing to be clothed in strength and dignity, and even more amazing to know that I can rejoice in the days to come because I have God as my protector and guide.

I find comfort in knowing that I am strong, courageous, full of wisdom, and that the time that I devote to God will bring me much added joy. I can truly laugh because I know who I am and whose I am in God. I know the power that God planted within me and I carry it everywhere I go.

Prayer

Lord, thank You for Your love and guidance. Continue to shape and mold me to be a woman of virtue with noble character. Continue to provide me with the strength, knowledge, and wisdom to meet the needs of my family. During unexpected times of change, I declare and decree that I will have no fear for I know You are with me. Teach me to speak with wisdom. Help me to be watchful and not indulge in ungodly activities and conversation. May my children call me blessed and cherish me as a mother but also as a woman who honors You, Lord. Amen.

LeAnn Cerise Hendrick

Day 4

"Be anxious for nothing, but in everything by prayer and supplication, with thanksgiving, let your requests be made known to God; and the peace of God, which surpasses all understanding, will guard your hearts and minds through Christ Jesus."
Philippians 4:6-7 NKJV

Life often presents us with seemingly insurmountable, God-sized problems. In our attempts to navigate these challenges alone, we unknowingly shift our focus from God. A small seed of concern can quickly blossom into a towering oak tree of overwhelming anxiety in our minds. Did you realize that the real battleground is our minds? Doubt and fear take root, and hopelessness leads us to agree with the enemy's whispers of defeat. But there is good news! God's Word in Philippians 4:6-7 is a powerful key to walking victoriously.

As children of God we possess the mind of Christ, but it requires cultivation through time spent with Him. We are instructed to boldly pray about everything, humbly presenting our needs and desires to God. Even amidst life's storms, we are called to express gratitude for His blessings and provision. This obedience unlocks His peace—a peace that transcends human understanding. It's an invitation to release our burdens and place them at His feet.

Consider the Proverbs 31 woman. She faced trials with a victorious mindset, refusing to let worry consume her. Instead, she turned to God in deliberate, specific prayer offered with humility and gratitude. She understood that true strength resides not in her own abilities but in God's unwavering presence.

This victorious mindset is a mind transformed by Christ, choosing faith over fear. Every thought presents a choice: captivity to doubt or obedience to Christ. 2 Corinthians 10:5 reminds us to bring every thought captive. This requires active, daily renewal of our minds.

This surrender isn't a one-time event but a daily commitment to walking closely with God and allowing His Word to reshape our thinking. When those familiar "what if" whispers arise, we counter them with the unwavering truth of God's promises.

Like the Proverbs 31 woman, we claim victory through intentional connection with God and the surrender of our thoughts to Christ. Begin your day with heartfelt gratitude. A thankful heart pleases God and makes it difficult for defeating thoughts to take root. Your Heavenly Father longs to hear your faith-filled prayers and offers you peace in exchange.

Prayer

Dear Lord, I pray for a renewed mind, transformed by Your truth. Help me take every thought captive to the obedience of Christ, focusing on what is true, noble, right, pure, lovely, and admirable. I reject negative and destructive thoughts. Empower me to see myself as You see me: a conqueror in Christ. Help me approach every challenge with confidence in Your presence and victory. I declare I am victorious in Christ and will walk in that victory. Thank You for Your

promises, Your peace, and for renewing my mind. I trust in You and give You all glory. In Jesus' name, Amen.

Donna Yates

Day 5

"May the Lord repay you for what you have done. May you be richly rewarded by the Lord, the God of Israel, under whose wings you have come to take refuge."

Ruth 2:12 NIV

My sisters, let's talk about Ruth—not just as a woman in the Bible, but as a walking testimony of what it means to move in divine faith, unshakable confidence, undeniable credibility, and unwavering commitment. Ruth did not show up in Bethlehem with credentials, titles, or influence. She arrived with a yes in her spirit, a loyalty that would not bend, and a heart postured to follow God no matter the cost.

In Ruth 2:12, Boaz acknowledges Ruth's quiet strength. He speaks a blessing over her because of her heart posture. That is where real confidence lives—not in how loud you are, how perfect your plan is, or how others see you, but in how aligned your heart is with God.

Let us break down the four principles every Christian woman leader must carry like spiritual armor:

1. FAITH

Ruth had every reason to turn back. She lost her husband, was in a foreign land, and had no earthly security. But she stayed the course. Her faith was not just belief—it was action. She moved in faith. And so must you. Faith is trusting God when the details are fuzzy and the "how" is not in sight. It is waking up every day with a decision to say, "God, I trust You anyway."

2. CONFIDENCE

Ruth never begged for acceptance. Her confidence was not cocky—it was rooted. She knew who she was through her actions and her humility. Real confidence is not loud, it is secure. It is the kind of posture that says, "I do not need to compete. I know who is guiding me." When your confidence is grounded in the One who called you, your presence speaks before you do.

3. CREDIBILITY

Boaz saw her credibility. Everyone heard about her. Sis, credibility is built in the quiet. In the field. When nobody's watching. When you are consistent, when your yes is yes, and when your character does the talking. The kingdom needs women whose fruit backs up their gifts.

4. COMMITMENT

Ruth did not just commit to Naomi—she committed to a process, to a people, and to a purpose she had not fully seen. That is what real leadership looks like. You stay when it is not convenient. You show up when your flesh wants to hide. Your commitment to God's process builds the path to your promise.

Prayer

Father God, thank You for creating me with purpose, vision, and strength. Today, I choose to walk in FAITH even when I cannot see the full picture. I anchor my CONFIDENCE in who You are, not what I feel. Let my CREDIBILITY reflect Your character, and may my COMMITMENT never waver, even when the road is hard. I know I am called, chosen, and covered. I surrender my timeline for Your divine timing. Help me lead with grace, move with authority, and love with intention. In Jesus' name, Amen.

Coach Stephanie Johnson

Day 6

"God is within her, she will not fall; God will help her at break of day."
Psalm 46:5 NIV

In a world that often tries to define us by our circumstances, our relationships, or our roles, it's vital to remember the truth found in Psalm 46:5: "God is within her." This powerful declaration holds the essence of our identity. When we recognize that God resides within us, we begin to understand the limitless strength that we possess.

Life is filled with challenges and unexpected trials that can shake our confidence and make us question our worth. In those moments of uncertainty, we may feel like we're on the edge of despair. The presence of God serves as our anchor. When we face difficulties, it is not our own strength that sustains us, but rather the strength of the Almighty within us.

Consider Esther, who risked her life to save her people, or Ruth, who demonstrated unwavering loyalty and courage in the face of adversity. These women didn't rely solely on their circumstances; they relied on God. They understood that their strength came not from their situation but from their divine connection.

We are often expected to juggle multiple roles—caregiver, professional, friend, and more. The demands can be overwhelming. It's easy to forget that we don't have to navigate these responsibilities alone.

The second part of the verse speaks to God's timely help. This imagery is powerful. Dawn symbolizes hope, renewal, and new beginnings. Just as the sun rises each day, bringing light and clarity, God promises to help us when we need it most. No matter how dark the night feels, morning is always on the horizon.

In moments of despair, instead of succumbing to fear or anxiety, let us turn our gaze towards God. Each day, we can commit our worries to Him, seeking His guidance and strength. We can pray for the ability to see our challenges from His perspective, which often brings peace and understanding.

Prayer

Dear Heavenly Father,

Thank You for the strength of women, their resilience, and their unique gifts. I ask that You bless each woman with the courage to embrace her identity as Your daughter.

To know that she is wonderfully made, worthy of love, and filled with purpose. Help her recognize the power within her, rooted in Your presence. When she faces challenges, remind her that she is not alone. Surround her with Your comfort and grace, and grant her the strength to rise above any obstacles.

Empower her to be a source of encouragement and support to those around her. May she shine brightly in her relationships, reflecting Your love and kindness. Help her to uplift other women, fostering a spirit of unity and collaboration rather than comparison.

As she walks through each day, remind her that Your plans for her are good. Fill her with hope and anticipation for the future, knowing that You have a purpose for every season of her life.

In Jesus' name, I pray, Amen.

Evangelist Krystal K. Ryan

Day 7

"The Lord will fight for you; you need only to be still."
Exodus 14:14 NIV

Life often brings battles that feel overwhelming—situations where I feel powerless, exhausted, and unsure of what to do next. In these moments, Exodus 14:14 is a powerful reminder that I don't have to fight alone. The Lord Himself goes before me, stands beside me, and fights on my behalf. My role is not to strive in my own strength but to trust in His.

When the Israelites stood at the edge of the Red Sea with the Egyptian army closing in, fear and uncertainty surrounded them. But God, in His faithfulness, made a way where there seemed to be none. He didn't ask them to figure it out—He simply asked them to be still and trust Him. That same promise holds true for me today.

I don't have to carry every burden, solve every problem, or fight every battle on my own. Instead of being consumed by anxiety or rushing to control everything, I can rest in God's power. He sees what I cannot, knows what I do not, and is always working for my good. When I surrender my battles to Him, I trade my exhaustion for His peace and my striving for His strength.

This verse challenges me to let go of fear, frustration, and doubt. Being still doesn't mean doing nothing—it means standing firm in faith knowing that God is actively working behind the scenes. Even when I don't see immediate change, I can trust that He is moving. My victory is not in my efforts but in His power.

Today, I choose to release my worries and let God fight for me. Whether I am facing difficulties in my personal life, business, or relationships, I will not allow fear to take over. I will stand still in faith, knowing that my God is faithful and He will make a way.

Prayer

Lord, thank You for being my defender and fighting on my behalf. When I feel overwhelmed, remind me that I don't have to strive in my own strength—You are already at work. Help me to be still, trust in Your plan, and walk in faith knowing that You are always in control. In Jesus' name, Amen.

Melissa Duran

Day 8

"God is within her, she will not fall; God will help her at break of day."
Psalm 46:5 NIV

I'll never forget the day my world was turned upside down. It was 2015, and I had just been diagnosed with Graves' disease. I thought I was living my best life, but unbeknownst to me, I was a ticking time bomb, waiting to unleash a storm of symptoms that would leave me feeling helpless and afraid.

But in the midst of that chaos, God was present. I remember feeling His peace, His comfort, and His reassurance, even when everything around me seemed to be falling apart. It was as if He was saying, "I've got this. I'm with you, and I'll help you through this."

As I looked to God's Word for comfort, I was reminded of Psalm 46:5, which says, "God is within her, she will not fall; God will help her at break of day." These words became my lifeline, my reminder that God was with me, even in the darkest of times.

The phrase "God will help her at break of day" particularly stood out. It reminded me that God's help is always available, always on the horizon. Even when the night seems darkest, the break of day is always coming, bringing with it the promise of new life, new hope, and new help.

As I spent time in the Word and in prayer, I began to trust God in a way I never had before. I learned to rely on His presence, His peace, and His power to get me through even the toughest of times.

If you're going through a chaotic time in your life, I want to encourage you to hold on to the promise of Psalm 46:5. Remember that God is with you, even when everything around you seems to be falling apart. He will help you, and His help is always available, always on the horizon.

Take a moment to reflect on the times in your life when you felt like God was present. How did you feel? What did you learn from those experiences?

Prayer

Dear God, thank You for being our rock, our refuge, and our strength. Thank You for being present with us, even in the midst of chaos. Help us to trust in You, to rely on Your presence, and to hold on to the promise of Your help. Amen.

Minister Regina Amos

Day 9

"Cast your burden on the Lord, And He shall sustain you; He shall never permit the righteous to be moved."
Psalm 55:22 NKJV

Many times, we are overcome by the burdens of life, situations that cause us deep anguish and trouble our hearts. Responsibilities and uncertainties plague us every waking moment. These are the nights when we can hear ourselves crying out in our anxiety and pain. We know we should trust God, we say we trust God, we even sing about trusting God, but letting go of burdens is easier said than done.

Trusting God and casting our cares on Him requires us to have faith, and faith requires letting go and stepping aside. Many of us pray but will not release, we continue to hold on to what we were never meant to carry by ourselves. "Cast your burden" means to trust God with our worries and anxieties instead of trying to take care of them ourselves. We are to release control and let God have His way. We are to rely on God's care and strength.

The act of casting cares on God is much like fishing. Casting our fishing line into the water is intentional surrender with the expectation of there being a fish on the other end.

David was the man after God's own heart, yet he was well acquainted with betrayal and sorrow and knew the pain of a troubled heart. David was a man who knew where to turn for strength, into the open arms of God who listens, cares, and sustains. God surely will provide and sustain those who trust in Him and Him alone. God will not abandon us in our time of need. God is the only one strong enough to carry our pain.

As He did with David, God expects us to bring our raw, unfiltered emotions to Him. David brought "his" to God in the evening, in the morning, and at noon. He prayed and cried out loud. David knew that God heard his every sigh, every tear, and every sorrowful unspoken word; and God will hear ours, too, but we must release our burden as an act of intentional surrender and voluntary release, totally trusting in the Father.

God does not promise that our life will be pain free and that we do not have to be consumed by sorrow. We can trust God to uphold us in our suffering and know He will never allow us to be shaken beyond what He can uphold. Call on Him today, release your burden, and rest in His sustaining power.

Prayer

Father God, I cast my burdens on You with great expectations. Amen.

Coach Renita Crump

Day 10

"...My grace is sufficient for thee."
2 Corinthians 12:9 KJV

In December 2022, after more than 21 years of suffering intermittently with crippling pain, debilitating nausea, countless visits to specialists, three major surgeries, many visits to the emergency room including a few ambulance rides, too many medications to name, having hands laid on me by some mighty men and women of God, and enough tears to swim in, my family and I found ourselves planning my funeral. We contacted some of our family and closest friends and we began to get visits from all over. Some flew in and some drove in, but they came not to say good-bye, but rather to pray that God would raise me up. Heaven was bombarded on my behalf!

During one of those visits, as others were praying for my healing, I heard the devil ask me, "What if you don't die? You've made all these people waste their time and money coming to see you." Without revealing the battle in my mind, I said to him, "Then I'll keep declaring the works of the Lord." He didn't realize it, but he was speaking life over me!

Just a few days later, on December 28, 2022, I felt the spirit of death rise from me, pack his bags and get out of my home. That may sound strange, but just as I knew I was dying, I now knew that I would live. I was overjoyed because I was certain that God was indeed going to heal me. Can you imagine my disappointment when weeks later I still felt sick? I simply could not understand why He kept me here but did not heal me. He was silent.

Two weeks later, God sent my answer through my Overseer. In the middle of her message, she said these words, "God wants somebody to know that all you have is a thorn in your flesh. You can still do what He's called you to do." Then, she went right back to ministering the Word.

That message led me to study 2 Corinthians 12:9 where God tells Paul, "My grace is sufficient for thee" in response to the third time Paul asked Him to remove his thorn. God wanted Paul to know that His grace was enough to get him through the thorn. Paul heard and believed God. From that moment on, what was a curse, Paul realized was a 'gift of a handicap' (MSG). That handicap kept Paul dependent on Jesus! As a result, Paul's ministry was second to none and he never mentioned that thorn again. If God's grace was enough for Paul, surely it's enough for my gift of a handicap.

Prayer

Father, today I pray for those who are dealing with handicaps that seem to be overwhelming and hindering their lives. I pray that just as You changed my perspective, change theirs. May they see the sufficiency of Your grace in all things. In Jesus' name we pray and believe that it is so. Amen and amen.

Pastor Patricia Salusbury

Day 11

Wisdom Is a Lady

"Wisdom cries aloud in the street, in the markets she raises her voice; at the head of the noisy streets she cries out; at the entrance of the city gates she speaks."
Proverbs 1:20-21 ESV

Wisdom is not hidden—it speaks loudly and boldly to those willing to listen. A true woman of wisdom, like a Mother in Zion, embodies the grace and strength found in the Word of God. She takes counsel from the wise, walking in discipline and integrity. She learns to be a godly wife—not quarrelsome or overbearing—understanding that peace builds a strong home (Proverbs 21:9). She is poised and self-controlled, even in the presence of kings (Proverbs 23:1-2).

This woman has spiritual street smarts. She resolves conflicts with fairness (Proverbs 18:18), avoids unwise financial entanglements (Proverbs 6:1-3), and humbles herself when correction is needed. She knows the power of her words—choosing soft answers that turn away wrath, rather than stirring anger (Proverbs 15:1). She guards her mouth, listens well, and speaks healing words that build up rather than tear down (Proverbs 12:18; 21:23; 26:4).

As a mother, she trains her children in righteousness, ensuring they walk the path of wisdom from an early age (Proverbs 22:6). She supports her husband in disciplining with love and guidance, aiming to raise children who bring peace and joy, not sorrow (Proverbs 19:18).

She observes the diligence of the ant and rejects laziness. She works with foresight and purpose, storing up provision in due season (Proverbs 6:6-8). She does not give in to idleness or fall prey to schemes that promise quick riches, knowing instead that wealth built steadily through honest labor lasts (Proverbs 13:11). Her labor is not just for gain—it is her worship.

Prayer

Lord, Your Word tells us that wisdom holds long life in one hand and riches and honor in the other. Help me embrace her ways and heed her voice. Grant me the grace of Your Holy Spirit to learn with clarity, retain with ease, and speak with wisdom. May my life reflect Your truth and glorify Your Son, Jesus Christ. Amen.

Mother in Zion Judy A. Wyndham

Day 12

Do not be anxious about anything, but in every situation, by prayer and petition, with thanksgiving, present your requests to God.
Philippians 4:7 NIV

Stress is an inevitable part of life. It appears differently in everyone. When our bodies feel threatened, it shifts into fight-or-flight mode. Stress often disguises itself, making it difficult to manage. Learning to manage stress is essential for maintaining physical and mental well-being.

As women we are taught to take care of others, be strong, and serve as the backbone of our families. I watched women, including myself, wear this persona as if nothing ever bothered us. I am a magnet for problems—people sought my advice, and I absorbed their issues like a sponge. Saying no wasn't part of my vocabulary. Regardless of how I felt, I maintained that role of always wanting the best for everyone. I wore the "I have it all under control" outfit daily. In reality, I was a dressed-up mess. Looking back, I was often one word away from falling apart because of stress. The outfit was not removed until I was behind closed doors where I would finally fall apart—only to get up the next day and do it all again.

One day, I noticed abnormal spikes in my heartbeat and pulse. My numbers would stabilize when I was still, but the moment I stood up, they rose again. My blood pressure ranged from 142/80 to 156/80. I felt light-headed and my chest was tight. After further evaluation, I learned I was experiencing anxiety and panic attacks, all related to stress. My blood pressure was so high that I had to stay at the doctor's office until it returned to a safer range. During a long conversation with my physician, I realized how deeply stress had infiltrated every area of my life.

When your woman's intuition tells you, "Sit down or get knocked down," you should listen. Unfortunately, I had unintentionally chosen the latter. Philippians 4:7 reminds us: Do not be anxious about anything, but in every situation, by prayer and petition, with thanksgiving, present your requests to God.

As I drove home, I prayed to God for the courage to speak up and let go. Something had to change because I was emotionally and mentally drained. The decision was made —I would no longer take on the problems of others. I began setting boundaries in every aspect of my life. Breaking old habits isn't easy, but I am more determined than ever to be my priority. My blood pressure is now 122/78. Managing stress is a necessary survival tool. Everyone's problem is not your problem. When I'm unsure of saying no I now say, "Let me pray about it and I'll get back to you."

Prayer

Lord, I thank You for another day. Give me the strength to change the things I can and the wisdom to accept the things I can't. I am blessed and honored knowing I can bring all my cares to You and rest! Amen.

Dr. JoAnne Hayes

Day 13

"The LORD is close to the brokenhearted and saves those who are crushed in spirit."
Psalm 34:18 NIV

Trauma has a way of leaving deep impressions on our hearts and minds. Whether it stems from loss, betrayal, abuse, or unexpected hardships, the weight can feel unbearable. Many of us carry wounds from our past, some visible and others hidden deep within. But no matter how broken we feel, God sees, He knows, and He cares.

Healing from trauma is not an overnight process. It requires surrender, trust, and patience. Often, we want to suppress our pain, pretending it doesn't exist or pushing forward without dealing with it. But true healing happens when we invite God into our broken places and allow Him to restore what was lost.

Steps to Healing Through Faith

1. Acknowledge the Pain – It's okay to not be okay. Jesus Himself experienced deep sorrow and grief. In the Garden of Gethsemane, He cried out in agony. God is not afraid of our emotions; He welcomes our honesty. Bring your pain before Him in prayer.

2. Surrender the Hurt to God – Trauma can cause us to put up walls, but healing begins when we surrender our burdens to the Lord. 1 Peter 5:7 says, "Cast all your anxiety on Him because He cares for you." Let go and trust that God is working even when you can't see it.

3. Renew Your Mind with Scripture – Trauma distorts our perception of ourselves and the world. The enemy wants to keep us trapped in fear and pain, but God's

word brings renewal. Meditate on scriptures that remind you of His love, His promises, and His power to heal.

4. <u>Seek Godly Support</u> – You are not meant to heal alone. God places people in our lives to support us—pastors, counselors, and trusted friends. Seek out a faith-based support system that can uplift and encourage you. Join a church family, www.ladiekisha.com for spiritual life coach guidance. Google is your friend search for therapists read their bio to see if they are someone you want to talk with.

5. <u>Walk in the Healing God Provides</u> – Healing is a journey, but each step forward is a victory. Celebrate the small wins. Know that God is restoring you day by day, bringing beauty from the ashes. Isaiah 61:3 promises, "He gives beauty for ashes, the oil of joy for mourning, the garment of praise for the spirit of heaviness."

Prayer

Heavenly Father, I bring my trauma and pain before You. I don't want to carry this burden alone. I ask for Your healing touch, Your peace that surpasses all understanding, and the strength to move forward in faith. Thank You for being close to the brokenhearted. I trust You to restore what was lost and bring wholeness to my soul. In Jesus' name, Amen.

Evangelist Laticia Cunnigham

Day 14

"I can do all things through Christ who strengthens me."
Philippians 4:13 NKJ

Life often brings moments that challenge my understanding. I've faced many things in my life, but most recently, I was hospitalized after having a mild stroke. Doctors ran an MRI and CT scan, and the test results revealed that I had Moya Moya disease. Fear ran through my mind because I didn't know what this disease was. Moya Moya is a rare disease that affects blood vessels in the brain, major blood vessels that carry oxygen to the brain and internal carotid arteries get narrower over time and eventually the brain does not get enough oxygen. To make up for the loss of oxygen, new blood vessels form near the base of the brain. These blood vessels are tiny and tangled. On a brain scan they look like puffs of smoke. Moya Moya gets worse over time and the lack of oxygen to the brain can cause strokes and seizures. Medications help to manage symptoms, but surgery is the only way to restore blood flow to the brain.

Receiving this diagnosis sounds scary but I must remember who's ultimately in control of all things. God is my healer and there's power in prayer. It's time to make some healthy choices and lifestyle changes. I'm going to start walking more and eating better because this will ultimately help with this disease. I want to live a healthy lifestyle, not just for me but for my kids and grandbabies. This will show them that doing hard things pays off and that all things can be done through Christ who strengthens us.

Prayer

Lord, thank You for Your promises that I can stand on and use as a weapon of warfare. I know I'm walking in victory and with Jesus by my side all things are possible. There's nothing too hard for the Lord. In Jesus' name, Amen.

Christina Aguilar

Day 15

"Trust in the Lord with all your heart, And lean not on your own understanding; In all your ways acknowledge Him, And He shall direct your paths."
Proverbs 3:5-6 NKJV

I blend "God" and "confidence," to remind myself daily that any and all confidence that I have is not in or of myself, but having an unwavering trust and confidence in God's Power– His Promises, Presence, Character, and Faithfulness. It's not self-confidence but a deep assurance that comes from knowing and acknowledging that God is in control, He is with me, strengthening and helping me, and directing my path, even when I can't see it.

"For we walk by faith, not by sight"
2 Corinthians 5:7 NKJV
"... faith is the substance of things hoped for, the evidence of things not seen." Hebrews 11:1 NKJV

So, how did I develop this faith and trust? I certainly did not start off believing God's Word right away! "Because of your unbelief; for assuredly, I say to you, if you have faith as a mustard seed, you will say to this mountain, 'Move from here to there,' and it will move; and nothing will be impossible for you" Matthew 17:20 NKJV.

In my disbelief, Jesus made a way–His promise to know Him intimately as I spent precious moments in His presence. By reading my Bible and immersing myself in His Word, He revealed His character, promises, and faithfulness to me. I was blessed with a Spirit-filled devotional (similar to the one you are reading now!) that not only deepened my understanding but also taught me practical application of His Word in my daily life. I was eventually led to a church community, a woman's bible study class and fellowship with like-minded sisters in Christ.

During this journey, I came to realize that I was created with a purpose. I realize now, why at a young age, God gifted me with artistic creativity, a passion for sketching, design, and sewing. It eventually led me into a season of thirty plus years in fashion merchandising, management, display, and interior design which was the foundation of opening my own store. I recognized that this creativity was not just for me but was a way to glorify the Lord and promote local artists in the community, too. This opportunity reflected God's goodness, His Love and inspired others! He opened another door for me to serve eight years in the Children's Ministry–creating arts and crafts reflecting Jesus' character through an etiquette class and teachings on the Fruit of the Spirit.

Even when I had not known God yet in my younger days, He was directing my steps!

I am blessed to share testimonies of His faithfulness, encouraging others to trust Him!

Prayer

Father, I put my trust in You, knowing that You hold my future! Help me walk boldly in "Godfidence" knowing I am Your daughter- loved, chosen, blessed, empowered by Your Spirit to glorify Jesus' name, Amen!

Isabelle Ramos

Day 16

"Behold, I will do a new thing, Now it shall spring forth; Shall you not know it? I will even make a road in the wilderness And rivers in the desert."

Isaiah 43:19 NKJV

The weight of the world can sometimes feel like a suffocating whirlwind on the hottest summer day, stripping away our very breath, leaving us sunburned and weary. We've all walked through those dry seasons of life – the broken relationships that cut deeper than any blade, the job loss that shatters our future security, the grief that leaves us feeling barren. In those moments, joy and peace have vanished, leaving only the desolate expanse of "what was" and the terrifying "what lies ahead."

And yet, in the heart of this desolation, a still, small voice whispers – a promise that shatters the torment of despair. "Behold, I will do a new thing." It's not a distant hope or flaky promise. It's an active declaration. God is about to disrupt the very fabric of our hopelessness.

"Now it shall spring forth; shall you not know it?" This isn't a passive suggestion. It's a challenge, a gentle but firm tug on our hearts. Are we so bogged down by our disappointments that we can't see Spring emerging right before our very eyes? God's asking us to look, truly look, beyond the immediate pain and recognize the signs of His intervention.

"I will even make a road in the wilderness and rivers in the desert." This visual is breathtaking. Roads where there was only visible sands, rivers where there was only cracked earth with no signs of life. Think of the impossible – a path carved through the chaos, refreshment where there was only thirst. This isn't just a metaphor; it's a promise of transformative change. It speaks to the heart of those moments when we feel utterly lost, when every direction seems blocked.

Perhaps you've been carrying the weight of past failures, the echoes of "you're not good enough" ringing in your ears. God says, "I am making a new road." He's clearing a path, erasing the old mistakes, and paving the way for a future filled with purpose. Or maybe you're facing a dryness in your spirit. God says, "I am bringing rivers where my love and peace overflows." He's not placing a bandaid on the old; He's creating something entirely new, beautiful, and unexpected. And He's inviting us to be a part of it.

Prayer

In the midst of my weary desert, I am holding on to Your promise even by a thread. I admit there are times where the dryness of circumstances I often find myself in has blinded me to the possibilities You hold. Forgive me for any uncertainty that has entered my heart. I release any residue of my past and lay them at Your feet.

Thank You, Lord, for doing a new thing in my life where my future is overflowing with purpose. In Jesus' name, Amen.

Sonja Sells

Day 17

"For I know the thoughts that I think towards you, says the Lord, thoughts of peace and not of evil, to give you a future and a hope."
Jeremiah 29:11 NKJ

I'm creating a memorial in my heart in remembrance of what God has delivered me from. There was a time when I thought darkness was going to swallow me up and there was no hope for me. The pain of my past abortions left me with shame, guilt, fear, anxiety, and depression. I never thought I would make it to my 40th birthday-yet here I am almost 47 years old. God has brought me through time and time again and I stand on his promises.

For so long, I've been in a waiting season for God to deliver on His promises. It seems like it's forever but healing, deliverance, and restoration don't always happen at once, sometimes it's a process and we must trust God's timing. I have a story to tell about God's goodness and faithfulness. God has truly healed my heart from my past abortions. When I turned 18, I had my very first one. I was too scared to tell my dad, and with the lack of support from the baby's father I didn't want to become a teenage statistic. It seemed like every two years, like clockwork, I was pregnant by the same guy and opted for an abortion. What was wrong with me? Didn't I learn my lesson the first time? I lacked the knowledge, guidance, and support that a mother figure might have provided. I tried to use birth control, but was never consistent and it caused the cessation of my periods, so I stopped taking oral contraceptives including the Depo Provera shot, which caused most of my hair to fall out and never grow back.

God has taken the pain and regret of my past abortions and has used my story to help other women know they're not alone and get free from the guilt and shame that often lingers long after an abortion. He's taken the good, the bad, and the ugly and formed something beautiful. Healing is possible with God. He never leaves us the way He finds us. He always has something so much better in store for those who love Him. I can't wait to see what God will do next in my life. I plan to stay on course and wait on God's timing and the many promises He has for me.

Prayer

God has a plan and purpose for our lives and I pray that you trust His timing and let Him write your story. He's faithful to complete what He started and will never leave nor forsake us. To God be the glory, In Jesus' name, Amen.

Cristina Alaniz

Day 18

"Trust in the Lord with all your heart and lean not on your own understanding; in all your ways submit to him, and he will make your paths straight."

Proverbs 3:5, 6 NIV

I have felt the icy grip of death three times. Three moments when my life hung in the balance, when my breath was stolen and my future seemed to dissolve before my eyes. The fear was suffocating. My mind screamed for answers: Why is this happening? Where are You, God? And yet, in those terrifying moments, I discovered the kind of trust that shakes the foundations of fear. Not a shallow, convenient faith, but a desperate, raw, all-consuming surrender to the only One who holds life and death in His hands.

The first time I faced death, I pleaded for understanding. My heart wrestled with doubt, and my soul clung to the edge of faith. I begged God for clarity, for control. But He didn't give me answers—He gave me Himself. And that was enough. When I finally let go of my frantic need to understand, He led me through the valley, step by step, breath by breath.

The second time, I was stripped of the illusion that I could navigate this life on my own. I had no choice but to trust Him completely. When I did, I experienced a peace so profound that it silenced the chaos around me. I saw that trust is not about knowing the outcome—it's about knowing the One who holds it.

By the third time, I no longer asked, Why me? I lifted my hands and said, God, I trust You. This was not resignation; it was power. It was the unshakable confidence of a woman who had seen God move time and time again. He had proven himself faithful. He turned my pain into purpose, my terror into testimony.

Sisters, I know what it means to be afraid. I know what it means to question if God sees you, if He hears you, if He even cares. But let me tell you—He is closer than your next breath. He is working in ways you cannot see. He is making your path straight, even when it feels like you are walking blind.

Prayer

Heavenly Father, I come before You, lifting up every woman reading this today. Lord, You see her heart, her fears, her struggles, and the moments where doubt tries to take hold. Remind her that she does not have to carry the weight of the unknown because You are already making her path straight.

Give her the courage to surrender, the strength to trust You fully, and the faith to walk boldly in Your divine purpose. When life shakes her, let her be rooted in the unshakable truth of Your love. When fear whispers, let her hear Your voice louder.

In Jesus' mighty name, in the name of Yeshua, Ase, and Amen.

Dr. Regina A. Turner

Day 19

"But they that wait upon the LORD shall renew their strength; they shall mount up with wings as eagles; they shall run, and not be weary; and they shall walk, and not faint."

Isa 40:31 ESV

I can remember several years ago I was waiting on God to fully manifest my purpose in Him. I was on a path that did not seem fulfilling. I felt like I did everything in my power to move forward but my strength was failing. So, I began to cry out before the Lord. I was hearing the voice of God, but the wait on becoming a Prophetess was unbearable. So, I began to fast and pray before the Lord. There is power and liberty in prayer. It liberated me through the power of intercession.

I heard Him in a still, small voice. "Wait on the Lord! Wait on the Lord." I swiftly gathered myself together and searched the Bible for scriptures that spoke of waiting on the Lord! I searched and found several but the one that was imperative and stood out the most in my spirit was Isa 40:31. "But waiting on the Lord in all things and counting on Him while you are waiting, He will renew your strength."

The strength that comes from God will help me keep going through the most difficult times. The strength while waiting gave me the courage to keep pushing, to keep going to the next level while I waited on God's timing. Courage helped me develop and gave me the assurance that He was there with me while I was waiting. God's heavenly work will surely come to pass. God showed me He will make up for the rest while I was trusting and believing in Him.

I shall mount up with wings like an eagle. The mounting up, the lifting, will cause me not to be weary in well doing. God gave me the grace to be that Proverbs 31 woman. God made up for the rest. God was working this out on my behalf. When I felt that quicken in my spirit! I said, "Thank you, Lord for renewing me while on the path. I shall not faint!"

Isa 40:31 keeps me striving, despite what is going on in my circle, my family, and in the marketplace or ministry. I am not weary in well doing. I am building while waiting on the Lord.

Prayer

Lord, I thank You for the timing of Your promise. Even when I became weary in well doing, You were there, Lord. When the reality of my circumstances was unclear you were renewing my strength. God, you gave me courage. You allowed my wings to mount up like eagles until the day of the manifestation of Your promise. I give You thanks for Your promise. In Jesus' name, Amen.

Prophetess Margaret D. Kirk

Day 20

"If I only touch His cloak, I will be healed."
Matthew 9:21 NIV

Many years ago, I was diagnosed with breast cancer with only 3 months to live. My life flashed before me. I was so devastated and angry with God, crying and asking Him, why me? All I ever wanted was happiness. All I ever did was serve Him and be a good mother. And now I'm dying? Why God!? Who's going to love my children like me? I felt that life had been nothing but unfair. I was in fear of dying, who wouldn't be? I didn't want to die. Again, I questioned God. Why me?

After the news, I ran to a church building and cried at the altar on my knees, praying and asking God to take the heaviness and sadness away from me. The burden was piercing my soul and heart deep like knives cutting me within. I did not want my little children and family to see me cry. It is okay to be sad and fearful, we are human. During a time of sadness and weakness we have to call on God, and no one else, for His strength and empowerment. I was asking for forgiveness. After all, I was going to be in heaven with Him. I knew at that moment I must live righteously.

After realizing that God chose me to be in His Kingdom, I submitted my whole heart to God. I wanted to be healed. My fear, anger, discouragement, and resentments were gone. It was all replaced with hope, joy, faith, obedience, and God's love. I chose to have chemotherapy, surgeries, and radiation to prolong my life and speak life-healing scriptures. Imagining myself touching Jesus' cloak as His power flowed through me to be healed in the supernatural realm. I was glowing with no hair, full of God's light and faith, giving hope and Jesus Christ to other cancer patients with only months to live. I was living here on this visible earth as it is in heaven, why wait? After 6 months of treatments, the doctors did a blood test and were dumbfounded- not a trace of cancer. God's word is yes and amen. The other cancer patients, doctors, and my family now believe in God. I am a walking miracle, a survivor of 26 years from only 3 months to live for eternity with Christ.

Prayer

Lord, thank You for Your scriptures and for Your promises. Your word is yes and amen. Teach me more of You and less of me as I walk through my valleys in obedience of unfailing faith. I will read more of Your scriptures, inscribe them in my heart, and stand firm and not uprooted as a palm tree. Knowing that no matter what comes my way, I shall withstand all storms as I walk on earth as it is in heaven. Amen.

Patricia Parada

Day 21

"For though we walk in the flesh, we do not war after the flesh: (for the weapons of our warfare are not carnal, but mighty through God to the pulling down of strong holds;) casting down imaginations, and every high thing that exalteth itself against the knowledge of God, and bringing into captivity every thought to the obedience of Christ."
2 Corinthians 10:3-5 KJV

In our journey as virtuous women, we are called to embody the character and principles of God, not just through our actions, but also through the intention and integrity of our hearts. The Scripture reminds us that while we navigate the trials of life—whether personal issues, family struggles, or spiritual battles—we are not alone, nor are we equipped with the same weapons as the world.

The passage serves as a powerful reminder that our true battle lies not in the physical realm, but in the spiritual. The weapons of our warfare are formidable tools given by God, designed for tearing down strongholds that cloud our perception of His truth. It is through prayer, the Word, divine love, and the empowerment of the Holy Spirit that we can confront and dismantle the strongholds in our lives.

So often, we may find ourselves battling thought patterns that hold us captive; doubts, insecurities, and fears that challenge our worth and impede our ability to forgive. These strongholds create a narrative that often contradicts the truth of who we are in Christ. Recognizing these thoughts as strongholds is the first step toward victory.

As daughters of the King, we have the assurance that we fight not for victory but from a place of victory. This perspective shifts our mindset significantly; it encourages us to approach challenges with confidence, knowing that the outcome is already secured by Christ's victory on the cross. This frame of reference empowers us to carry ourselves with a "woman of strength" mindset.

In moments of doubt or fear, let us remind ourselves of our identity as victors in Christ. We can reassess our thoughts and capture them—aligning them with God's truths, casting aside anything that exalts itself against His knowledge.

You are not alone in this fight; there is a community of women and believers standing shoulder to shoulder with you, praying and encouraging one another. Embrace your role as a warrior equipped with divine weapons. As we learn to implement God's strategies, know that you are part of His grand design, destined for victory and purpose.

Prayer

Father, I thank You for the powerful reminder that while I walk in the flesh, I do not wage war in the same manner. Help me to recognize and dismantle the strongholds in my life that stand against Your truth. Guide me to wield spiritual weapons; prayer, Your Word, love, and the power of the Holy Spirit with confidence and intention. May I always remember that I fight from victory, through Christ. In His name, I pray. Amen.

Lashon Dorsey

Day 22

"The fear of the Lord is the beginning of knowledge, but fools despise wisdom and instruction."

Proverbs 1:7 NIV

I have worked diligently to demonstrate my wisdom and knowledge in the various roles I have held, whether it be in a lab, a classroom, as a school leader, or as a caregiver in the community while working with patients as a medical professional. However, I've noticed that my wisdom and knowledge are sometimes not as valued as I hoped. It has sometimes brought shame, like the light of my wisdom would be dimmed thus bringing a feeling of loss and not knowing who I could trust or share my concerns.

Whether at your job, church, or school, we envision gaining knowledge through practice, learning from the wisdom of others, and seeking guidance from those who wish to share their experiences. Sadly, this is not always the case; there are times when people mock or devalue our gifts, making us feel ashamed like imposters regarding the talents we have been given. This is not the purpose we were created for. We must believe in what we are: children of God. He has placed us on this earth to carry out His work, having sacrificed His only Son so that we may live in grace and share our gifts with others.

Proverbs 1:7 reminds us, "The fear of the Lord is the beginning of knowledge, but fools despise wisdom and instruction. . We are not to feel ashamed when we earn a certificate, receive accolades, or acquire a promotion or degree. We must embrace that the knowledge we receive is a part of the desire for His wisdom and heed His instructions to be good stewards.

So, how do we move forward when we feel defeated, degraded, or unappreciated? We must seek God's discernment by pausing and listening. Listening can be challenging, especially for a woman balancing the responsibilities of being a wife, mother, daughter, and aunt. However, we need to take a moment for ourselves and understand that not everyone will recognize the goodness that comes from listening to God.

Today, I will take the time to reflect, read the Word, meditate on it, and listen for the direction of how I should share the acquired wisdom. I will abolish the thoughts of lack, use wisdom to fulfill the stewardship and move not in vain. I will embrace the fear of the Lord to empower, pivot, and bless someone else, and through this learning, I will become stronger from His instruction.

Prayer

Lord, I am open to receiving guidance from those who have my best interests at heart. Grant me the sage wisdom to embrace my self-worth and the discernment to apply my knowledge wisely in all situations. Walk beside me as I stand tall, accepting the wisdom You have given to me. Help me to walk with clarity and purpose, fulfilling my calling and aligning my steps with Your will. In Jesus' name, Amen.

Dr. Jewel White Williams

Day 23

"Even though I walk through the valley of the shadow of death I will fear no evil, for you are with me, your rod and your staff, they comfort me."

Psalm 23: 4 ESV

In 2014, I survived being in a fire. God opened my eyes on how important He is in my life. The fire caused me a lot of pain, on a scale of 1 to 10 it was a 10. I was blessed that the fire didn't burn my face, it went to my head. After this happened my faith and belief in God became stronger. During this time I refused to take the pain medication that the doctor prescribed. How was I able to deal with the pain? It was only God. I kept in mind the pain that Jesus endured—His suffering on the cross and how He overcame death—and that carried me through my healing process, from the fire to, more recently, when I battled shingles. His victory gave me strength to believe healing was possible for me, too. As a mother to four adult children and 3 grandchildren I knew God still had a purpose for me.

I live my life with a purpose of a positive mindset. My goal in life is to encourage others that no matter what you go through, God is the one that has the power to change it. My life is filled with the purpose that God has for me. He has led me to start a ministry board called Spoken Word Ministry and a homeless ministry called Evolution Homeless Ministry. Whether it's spreading a positive word to someone or helping someone in need, I truly believe that God has put it in my heart to be an encouragement to others.

Psalm 23 has had a significant impact on my life. When I am dealing with things that I don't know how to handle, I read Psalm 23. It gives me hope. It shows me how God can and will change my life, all I have to do is just trust and wait on His timing. His timing is perfect. I know that He has all the power to change things, nothing is too big or too small for our God. He can make the crooked path straight and when darkness is surrounding me He is the light that sees me through.

Prayer

Lord, I give You all of me, I give You everything that I have. I live my life for Your purpose and to do Your will. Nothing and no one will take me away from You. I will never let go of Your hand. I will always follow Your lead; where You go, I will go. My heart belongs to You, Lord God. Your word is inscribed on the tablets of my heart. I worship You in Spirit and in truth. Your praise will forever be on my lips. Thank you, Lord, for loving me. Amen.

Anita McAllister

Day 24

"Even though I walk through the darkest valley, I will fear no evil, for you are with me; your rod and your staff, they comfort me."
Psalms 23:4 NIV

In October 2018, Psalms 23 repeatedly came to me especially, verse 4. I would hear and see this scripture in my dreams. In many other places, like social media, stores, or websites, Psalms 23 would appear ironically. So, one day I called my mom explaining, "I keep hearing and seeing parts of Psalms 23." My mother said that God is warning and promising me that whatever I go through He will be there for me. The following month, in November, my life changed drastically. I slipped and fell on my job working as a Registered Nurse Manager at a long-term care facility sustaining multiple injuries; this was when my valley experience began.

One day my Heavenly Father asked me, "Do you know why the sun doesn't shine through the valley?" So, I began to explore, I found out that mountains produce long shadows. Mountains block most of the sunlight in the valley causing less light.

Part of the Psalms 23:4 reads: even though I walk through the darkest valley, I will fear no evil, for you are with me. Darkness tends to be fearful, but when light shines, the darkness disappears. Metaphorically, Jesus is light in the dark times in our lives; His light blinds the darkness. The rest of Psalms 23:4 reads, your rod and staff comfort me; metaphorically, the Holy Spirit guides and comforts us during difficult times.

While in the valley, you experience trials and tribulations. It's a place where your faith in God is tested!

When undergoing difficult times, God meets you where you are. I met my Heavenly Father on a deeper level in the valley, not knowing He was already waiting for me. Finding my way through this tough time was confusing and fearful. One afternoon, while praying and crying to God, I received a revelation that I stopped relying on Him for everything that concerned me. I asked God while praying, "What will I do now, nursing is my career?" God replied, "Nursing does not define you; I do."

The dark valley has turned me closer to God. I must testify that God is providing my needs for my family and my bills are being paid. I am no longer in control of my life, it's God; He is my guide for each step of my life. The Holy Spirit is my comforter for when I get weary about bills, health, and the unknown of tomorrow. I will continue to trust God, knowing that He will turn my valleys of darkness into valleys of blessings.

Prayer

Dear Heavenly Father,

I come to You today with gratitude and repentance in my heart! As I go through difficult times, give me the strength and faith knowing, if You allow the valley experience, then I will come out victoriously. In Jesus Christ's mighty name, Amen.

Kojuvona Telfair-Singleton

Day 25

"In Everything you do, put God first, and He will direct you and crown your efforts with success!"
Proverbs 3:6 Living Bible

With the multiple obligations and duties of most women, you need to know, like never before, that God MUST be FIRST in your life. Yes, Daddy God must be FIRST before yourself, your husband, kids, church, business, and everything you do.

I truly need the Lord to guide me every single day as I travel along life's way, for I just can't make it by myself. I learned how exhausting it is to try to do it on my own and in my own strength. My sisters, you will discover, as I did, that no matter how gifted, creative, or strong you think God has made you, you will ALWAYS need Him-and need Him to be FIRST.

While going through life's storms and character-building experiences, I have learned the value of my personal devotional time with the Lord. It gives me supernatural strength, wisdom, peace, joy, direction, and understanding of what the heaven is going on. The Lord had to teach me how to stand when I didn't quite understand the journey. My prostrate prayer time in the mornings- laying at His feet to talk and listen to Him, my meditation of His Word daily, anointing myself with blessed oil and taking communion carried me through Stage 3 breast cancer and brought my husband Bishop Bolden home from COVID being on the ventilator for 35 days. Those practices carried us through his 62 day-hospital stay and 9 weeks of rehab. The doctors said three times he wasn't going to make it, but "By Jesus stripes we were HEALED AND ALL IS

WELL." (I said this 100 times daily by the leading of the Holy Ghost and God did it.)

When you learn the power and the amazing blessing of putting God FIRST, He will give you divine protection, divine direction, and divine connections. I always say, "God lead me where you need me." You cannot fail putting Him FIRST; you will never lose, you will never run out, and He will never let you go under.

We all desire to be FIRST in our lives, with our husband, children, businesses, etc. We want people to prioritize us. God likes to be praised and prioritized, too. In order to have a vibrant, exciting, prosperous, productive, resourceful, creative, and triumphant life, put God FIRST and watch how you will begin to Soar like never before for His Glory.

Prayer

Oh Father God in the name of Jesus, thank You. Thank You for the chance to get it right because my success is only in You. With joy and excitement starting today, I place You FIRST, to share my heart and to hear Yours. For you to divinely download into me wisdom, creative ideas, and instructions for the day to bring You glory. I now make FIRST things FIRST...You. Thank You for always being there for me, I love You.

Dr. Rhonda A. Bolden

Day 26

"Being confident of this very thing, that he which hath begun a good work in you will perform it until the day of Jesus Christ."
Philippians1:6 KJV

God created us to fulfill a purpose in the fabric of time.

Life is filled with swift transitions. Sometimes these transitions don't look like the path we expected to take to reach our goals. Sometimes they knock the wind out of us, take us off our square and cause us to doubt who we are, where we are going, and if we will ever really get there. We have all had a great vision we pursued until we hit a bump in the road or encounter challenges along the way that cause us to question our very existence, our purpose. These pitfalls we encounter do not change our purpose. Know that the bumps, challenges, and unexpected moments are all part of the journey. They are actually the friction needed to work out the gifts in us, cultivate our virtue as they pull and push us straight into our positions of victory.

In this verse we are reminded that we have no need to be discouraged or doubtful that we will make it to the end. Why? Because God has not set us up for failure because He can never fail. It is He who is doing the work in us and not we ourselves. We are His workmanship as stated in Ephesians 2:10 (ESV), "For we are his workmanship created in Christ Jesus for good work, which God prepared beforehand, that we should walk in them" and therefore every detail of our lives is strategically planned and put in place to produce something good in the end. God WILL finish what He started, all we have to do is fall in line.

I encourage you today to stand firm in adversity, in the confidence in God knowing our Father has already set us up to win! Know that we fight from victory not for victory. We don't fold in the battle, we do as 2 Timothy 2:3 (KJV) says –"Thou therefore endure hardness, as a good soldier of Jesus Christ."

Prayer

Father, as we go through this journey of becoming, we trust in Your plan for our lives. Thank You for the declared reminder that it is not us who does the work but it is You who does the work through us and as long as we partner with You and follow Your lead we will never fail.

Elder Dawn D. Braithwaite

Day 27

"I am the light of the world. Whoever follows me will never walk in darkness, but will have the light of life"

John 8:12 NIV

It's crazy how easy it is to live in darkness and not even know it until a glimpse of light touches your heart and fills it with peace, love, and joy. It feels so good from the inside out!

It's a trip how darkness seems to feel so good and consumes you. Some would call it the pursuit of happiness. The constant hustle for material things that offer temporary pleasure can be taken away at a blink of the eye: fame, cars, clothes, jewelry, drugs, alcohol, superficial friends, everything social media makes look glamorous and good. How can something that seems to bring so much happiness leave you so empty and always searching for something else? Because things are temporary and chasing after them to fulfill your soul will keep you on a never-ending road of emptiness. Happiness is situational, but joy comes from God and fulfills you from the inside out despite your circumstances.

What removes darkness? Light! Think about how awake you feel, warm and alive, when the sun rises from night to the day, or the sun breaks through a cloudy day and shines on you. You're reenergized, endorphins kick in and momentary happiness arises. Well, imagine having that sweet warmth inside of you all the time despite your circumstances. Imagine not just receiving the light but being the light. Jesus said, "I am the light of the world. Whoever follows me will never walk in darkness, but will have the light of life" John 8:12 NIV.

Imagine brightening up everyone's day when you walk into work shining, smiling, full of the joy and peace that only God can give. Imagine walking in diffusing problems, finding positive solutions, staying out of the madness and choosing to shine and be positive on purpose.

The day you choose God and choose to walk in His light and His love, God will walk with you. Be intentional with your walk with God and you will see your life change from the inside out.

It's your time to come out of the darkness and let your light shine. It's your turn to have a joy in your heart that no one can take away. It's your time to have God's unwavering love with you always. He is the light of the world! Life might be full of challenges, but imagine how amazing life will be knowing God, the light of the world, is with you, breaking through the darkness, dwelling in you, and giving you your own personal light to shine and spread His love. It's your time to shine! You got this!

Prayer

Father, Thank You for Your love, Your mercy, and Your grace and for giving us the opportunity to receive Your warm, sweet light. Removing us from darkness and shining in Your name!

Thank you for Your patience and forgiveness.

Amen.

Candice Bryant

Day 28

"Blessed is she who has believed that the Lord would fulfill his promises to her!"
Luke 1:45 NIV

Anna sat in the stillness on the floor of her prayer closet, surrounded by the sacred remnants of her journey—handwritten sticky notes, faded vision boards, and tattered journals. She revisited each dream with quiet reverence, reading the promises she had once boldly written in faith. Time passed, and some prayers remained unanswered, but her faith had not wavered. With each page turned and every vision remembered, she chose to believe again—rooted in trust, anchored in God, and fully confident that He was still creating her story.

Luke 1:45 resounds like a quiet anthem for women like Anna—for every woman faithfully carrying a vision, nurturing a family, serving in unseen spaces, or building something only heaven fully understands. "Blessed is she who believed..." Not because she had all the answers. Not because the results came quickly. But because she dared to believe in the waiting, trusting that God would be faithful to fulfill what He promised.

Elizabeth spoke this verse to Mary who had just said yes to the unthinkable—carrying the Son of God. Mary did not demand details or timelines. She did not negotiate the cost; she believed. That belief, even in the uncertainty, was counted as blessed.

This is the kind of faith God honors—not that waits for proof but that clings to the promise.

You may not be carrying a divine child, like Mary, but you are likely carrying something very sacred—a calling, a dream, a ministry, a message, a breakthrough that you know God has spoken to your heart. And maybe, like Anna, you have done everything right. You've prayed, planned, obeyed, and now you're waiting.

But do not mistake silence for absence. Do not confuse delay with denial.

God is still working—often most powerfully behind the scenes. Your belief is not in vain. He honors the woman who dares to believe when nothing around her yet confirms it.

The world rewards instant wins and visible results, but heaven blesses quiet endurance. The woman who stands firm in faith—when it's complex, hidden, or slow—carries the deepest form of strength.

You've been praying and waiting...
You've been sowing seeds of obedience without seeing harvest...
You've been trusting God through uncertainty...

If that's you today, let Luke 1:45 be your reminder to continue to speak life over the promise. You've come too far to stop believing now. Continue to worship while you wait. We should continue to believe that the God who made the promise faithfully fulfills it.

Prayer

Dear Heavenly Father, thank You for blessing me not only in fulfilling Your promises but also for reminding me that my faith pleases You. Lord, strengthen me when I become weary of waiting. Let my faith and trust in You remain unwavering and my heart anchored in Your promises. In Jesus' name, I pray, Amen.

Dr. LaTonya K. Poole

Day 29

"She opens her hand to the poor and reaches out her hands to the needy."

Proverbs 31:20 ESV

From the very genesis of creation, humanity was woven with the threads of divine intention. Fashioned in God's image, we were designed to reflect His heart – a heart overflowing with compassion, justice, and a profound love for the vulnerable. This isn't just a suggestion; it's a reflection of our original design, a blueprint etched onto our souls by the Master Architect Himself.

Yet, the journey of me living out this divine purpose was often met with opposition. The world, with its distractions, constantly caught me off guard to keep my attention from the Father, seeking to pull me away from the very essence of who I was created to be. The relentless pursuit of worldly gain can easily eclipse the gentle call to serve. These forces can obscure our vision, hindering us from extending the open hand and reaching out to those in need.

For me, this struggle took on a stark and unexpected form. The foundation of my world crumbled when my beloved husband was murdered, leaving me a young widow with two precious little girls to raise. In an instant, the life I knew vanished, replaced by a landscape of grief, uncertainty, and the daunting responsibility of single motherhood. My purpose, as I understood it then, felt shattered into a million pieces.

In the years that followed, a new path unfolded. Through the gift of song, I began to travel, sharing my voice and connecting with audiences. While there was a measure of fulfillment in this, persistent emptiness lingered. The applause and accolades couldn't fill the void left by loss, nor could they fully satisfy the deep yearning within me for something more profound. The tragedies that had darkened my doorstep – the sudden absence of my husband, the weight of raising my daughters alone – felt like insurmountable obstacles threatening to consume me.

One day, I stood at the altar, and it was in that quiet moment that the gentle whisper of God's original intent began to resurface. The words of Proverbs 31:20, once a verse I admired from afar, started to resonate with a new urgency. I realized that my own brokenness, my own experience of need, had the potential to birth a deeper empathy for others. The emptiness I felt was not meant to be a permanent state but a space for God's love to fill, a love that compels us outward.

Prayer

Father, We are still called to reflect Your heart, to extend compassion, and to be Your hands and feet in a world desperately in need of Your love. The path may be different than we envisioned, marked by unexpected turns and deep valleys, but the invitation to open our hands to the poor and reach out to the needy remains a constant beacon, guiding us back to the very essence of our creation.

In Jesus' name.

Pastor Sheila P. Ingram

Day 30

"Strength and dignity are her clothing, And she smiles at the future."
Proverbs 31:25 NASB

There is a place where the Proverbs 31 woman dwells—a cleft, a refuge carved by the hand of God where wisdom, strength, and grace converge. It is not just a position of safety but a launching place of purpose. In biblical imagery, a cleft is a sacred space, like the one where God placed Moses as His glory passed by (Exodus 33:22). The Proverbs 31 woman does not just exist; she abides in this cleft, wrapped in divine strength, adorned with dignity, and positioned for victory.

The world often misinterprets her identity, reducing her to an impossible standard or a checklist of accomplishments. But in reality, she is a warrior in the Spirit, a vessel of wisdom, a nurturer of destiny, and a carrier of the kingdom's mantle. Her strength is not her own—it is cultivated in the cleft, in the secret place of surrender, where God refines her into a victorious woman of purpose.

A Proverbs 31 woman does not emerge overnight. She is forged in the fire of refinement, shaped by trials, and strengthened in the secret place. To be "clothed with strength and dignity" is not merely poetic imagery—it is the armor of a woman who has learned to trust in the Lord despite the battles she faces.

The cleft represents a place of intimacy with God where He whispers strategies for victory. The enemy seeks to deceive women into believing that their strength comes from external achievements, but the Proverbs 31 woman knows better. She is victorious because she abides in Christ, the rock of her salvation.

Like Moses in the cleft, she understands that glory is revealed in surrender. She is not afraid of the future because she knows the one who holds it. She does not crumble under pressure because her foundation is built on faith. She is not defined by the expectations of the world but by the divine mandate placed upon her life.

Prayer

Heavenly Father, I come before You with a heart of gratitude, thanking You for the strength and dignity that You clothe me with daily. You have positioned me in the cleft of Your presence, a place of refuge and empowerment, where Your wisdom, grace, and purpose flow abundantly. Teach me to abide in You, to dwell in the secret place where my spirit is renewed and my purpose is refined, for my strength is found in You alone. When trials arise, let my heart remain steadfast, knowing that I am not alone—you are my fortress, my defender, and my guide. I surrender my heart, my journey, and my purpose to You, knowing that in the cleft of Your presence, I am victorious. In Jesus' name, Amen.

Dr. Prophetess Natasha Lawson

Bonus Day

"For I will restore health unto thee, and I will heal thee of thy wounds, saith the LORD."

Jeremiah 30:17 KJV

As a believer, I have experienced a plethora of faith tests such as believing God for a strategy to reduce my debt so that I could purchase my home as well as believing God for a promotion in my career. Additionally, I have encountered a faith test to believe God for my daughter's salvation. However, I would have to say that my greatest test of faith has been believing God for complete healing in my body.

Healing is defined as the process of making or becoming healthy or sound again. In order to receive the healing, I first must believe God's word. Furthermore, I must speak and pray His word daily over my body and keep it in my mind so that it penetrates my spirit man.

When I first received a medical diagnosis in December 2024, I wasn't afraid of what was next because I believed God's word that He took a whipping for my sickness on Calvary. On December 31, 2024, I vividly remember God telling me, "Daughter, this sickness is not unto death and you will live out the length of your days which is 90 years minimum to 120 years maximum." I find comfort in knowing and believing what God spoke to me on that day because I recorded it in my journal as well as read it daily.

Not only did God tell me that I would live and not die, He gave me a strategy that consisted of a holistic and medicinal health care plan. Specifically, God gave me the names of supplements to take daily, an exercise plan, and the medical practice who would take care of me during this time.

When I read the foundational scripture of my devotion, I am reminded that God has restored my health and healed my wounds. When I was in my mother's womb, every cell, organ, muscle, and tissue was divinely orchestrated and they were good. During my prayer time, God told me, "Rebecca, I have recalibrated your internal organs and realigned your body so that you are able to fulfill your Kingdom assignment."

As I come to the close of the devotion, I want to encourage you and remind you that healing is the children's bread. As I mentioned previously, receiving a health diagnosis is not a death sentence. Moreover, it's a daily opportunity for me to continue to fight the good fight of faith and declare "that I am the healed on this side of glory" and there is glory after this.

Prayer

Heavenly Father,

Thank You for being the God who heals, restores, and sustains. I stand in agreement with Your Word that healing belongs to Your children and that by the stripes of Jesus, I am already healed. Lord, I praise You for divine strategies, supernatural peace, and the assurance that every promise You have spoken over my life shall come to pass.

Prophetess Rebecca D. Huggins

Bonus Day

"I took hold of you from the ends of the earth, and called from its uttermost parts, and said to you, 'You are My servant– I have chosen you, not rejected you. Fear not, for I am with you, be not dismayed, for I am your God. I will strengthen you. Surely I will help you. I will uphold you with My righteous right hand."
Isaiah 41:9-10 TLV

When God calls you, you must have courage. It's a scary, yet humbling, but totally unnerving excitement for your new journey. From a very young age, I've always felt the presence of The Lord and His hand on my life, but didn't know why. I just knew God was always there.

Now that I am older and a born-again Believer, I know it is God who has called me and chosen me, just like He chose you. And with being called to do His will, I am not alone. God is with me to guide me, lead me with His eye and tell me what to say, how to say, and when to say it. All I have to do is be obedient.

My heart, my will, and my spirit are in a perpetual state of longing and saying yes to Jesus. He is my first love and my everything. I truly am nothing without Him. Isaiah 41:9-10, reminds me of how far God has called me from, all the bad places I found myself in and how He dug me out of all the pits I put myself in. Out of all the bad decisions, depression, and all my sins. He washed me clean and called me His own and never rejected me, even in my deliberate sin! God still loved me. God still wanted me and God still chose me. He never rejected me, but only redirected my path to Him and His righteousness. It is the Lord who will strengthen me and help me to do His will, for I am His servant, His beloved and He will never leave me nor forsake me. Our Father holds us in His righteous hand and will always be there to help and answer us when we call on His Name. He will always answer us. God's love is eternal.

Prayer

Father God, my life is Yours! I say yes a thousand times over, an eternal yes to You forever. Whatever Your will is, that is my command. Thank You for giving me the courage to obey You and do whatever it is You would have me to do and say what You want me to say. I am Yours and I agree with Your will for my life and pray to always stay humble and never lifted in pride and to give You all the glory, for it all belongs to You. In Jesus' name, Amen.

Minister Peshon Allen

Closing Prophetic Prayer

Virtuous & Victorious: 30 Day Devotional for the Proverbs 31 Woman

Heavenly Father,
We come before You in reverence, adoration, and awe, lifting up every woman who has journeyed through this devotional—each one uniquely called, divinely appointed, and fearfully and wonderfully made. Lord, we thank You for the seeds of wisdom, faith, and strength that have been sown during these 30 days. We seal every word, every scripture, and every revelation with the blood of Jesus.

Now, Father, in the matchless name of Jesus, I prophetically decree and declare that the Proverbs 31 Woman shall rise in full authority, clothed in dignity and robed in righteousness. I declare that she will walk in uncommon favor, unstoppable grace, and unwavering faith. She shall open her mouth with wisdom, and on her tongue will be the law of kindness. Her steps will be ordered by the Lord, and she will walk boldly into rooms where her name has already been whispered by Heaven.

Lord, release over her life divine strategies, kingdom blueprints, and supernatural downloads for wealth, health, purpose, and destiny. Let her house be filled with peace, her hands with productivity, and her heart with praise. As she builds, may she not grow weary. As she serves, may she be replenished. As she sows, may she reap in abundance—pressed down, shaken together, and running over

I cancel every assignment of the enemy sent to distract, delay, or discourage her. No weapon formed against her shall prosper, and every tongue that rises in judgment shall be condemned. She is more than a conqueror, crowned with wisdom, and saturated in the oil of joy. I speak to her inner woman—ARISE! ARISE in boldness, in beauty, in balance, and in brilliance. Arise as the intercessor, the nurturer, the leader, the entrepreneur, the wife, the mother, the warrior, and the worshipper.

I prophetically declare that her past will no longer define her, her pain will no longer confine her, and her fear will no longer silence her. She will speak, and mountains will move. She will pray, and heaven will respond. She will believe, and miracles will manifest. She will walk in victory all the days of her life, because the Lord her God is within her—she will not fail.

God, let Your favor be her shield and Your Word be her sword. Crown her with the oil of gladness, wrap her in garments of strength, and release upon her the fragrance of grace. Every generational curse is broken, and generational blessings are now activated. She is a kingdom ambassador, anointed to disrupt darkness, raise holy standards, and birth legacies for generations to come.

Lord, as she continues beyond these 30 days, let Your Spirit rest heavily upon her. Let her voice be amplified, her gifts be sharpened, and her territory enlarged. May she never settle for less than what You promised. May her heart burn for righteousness, her hands remain clean, and her faith remain fierce.

We thank You that she is not just virtuous, but victorious. She is not just refined, but she is rising. And she is not just anointed—she is appointed for such a time as this.

In the mighty and majestic name of Jesus Christ, Amen and Amen.

Prophetess Chaundra Gore

Afterword

As we bring this sacred journey to a close, let us reflect on the transformative power of faith, community, and the enduring example of the Proverbs 31 woman. Virtuous & Victorious: 30-Day Devotional for The Proverbs 31 Woman is more than a book —it is a divine movement of wisdom, love, and spiritual growth curated by the Holy Spirit through the hearts and pens of 34 women of God.

Each day, you were guided by scripture, devotion, and heartfelt prayer—crafted not from convenience but from conviction. These pages echo the lived experiences of women who, like you, are striving daily to walk in purpose, strength, and grace. From the depths of spiritual warfare to the heights of God's promises, every devotion in this book was written to awaken the virtuous woman within you and remind you that victory is already yours.

The Proverbs 31 woman is not a myth or unreachable standard—she is a reflection of God's divine design in motion. She is resourceful, resilient, and revered—not because she is without flaw, but because she is filled with faith. Her strength is anchored in her relationship with God. Her value is not found in perfection, but in her posture of praise, humility, and obedience. Through this devotional, we hope you were reminded that her story is your story. Her victories can be your victories. Her virtue is the same virtue God is birthing in you.

To the woman reading this: we honor your journey. We celebrate your progress and we affirm your future. You are seen. You are called. You are chosen. Whether you're standing in the middle of your breakthrough or still waiting on a promise to manifest, know that God is not finished with you. Every prayer whispered, every tear shed, and every act of surrender has not gone unnoticed by the Lord. He is faithful, and His word concerning you will not return void.

As you close this devotional, may it remain open in your heart. Revisit these scriptures. Reflect on these devotions. Pray without ceasing. And when doubt, fear, or discouragement tries to rise up, remember: You are a virtuous woman. You are a victorious woman. And you are walking in the fullness of your calling—gracefully, boldly, and faithfully.

On behalf of A Divine Collaboration and every woman who contributed to this work, thank you for allowing us to walk with you, day by day. May the seeds sown in this devotional blossom into a harvest of strength, courage, and spiritual maturity in your life. The journey doesn't end here. It only begins anew—with greater purpose, deeper faith, and unwavering trust in the God who made you.

Stay rooted in the Word. Stay covered in prayer. And above all, stay victorious.

In Christ's Love,

Prophetess Chaundra Gore

Co-Founder of A Divine Collaboration: The Virtuous & Victorious Sisterhood

Prophet Chaundra N. Gore is a Presidential Lifetime Award Recipient, an Affirmed Prophet, talk show host on The Act of Moving by Faith on Facebook LIVE & YouTube, Servant Leadership Strategist (20yrs U.S. Army Guard Reserve & Army Reserve), destiny catalyst, international speaker, faith-based motivational coach/trainer; #1 Amazon best-selling author, CEO of Lens of Faith Speaks Coaching and Consulting, Chancellor of Lens Of Faith Academy of Servant Leadership, and the Founder and President of Focused and Aligned Women's Business Empowerment Foundation Inc. She is a 100% disabled Army Veteran, as well as a Sexual Assault Victim Advocate, a member of Zeta Phi Beta Sorority Incorporated, a member Kappa Epsilon Psi Military Sorority Incorporated, a member of the National Society of Success and Leadership, and an advocate for Service members as a member of The Association for United States Army. Outside of her professional titles, she is a mother, a survivor of a suicide attempt, domestic violence, and sexual abuse.

Chaundra has a Bachelor of Science in Business Management. A Master of Science in Leadership. A Diploma in Antiterrorism Officer Basic Course (ATOBC). Currently a Doctoral Candidate at Grand Canyon University pursuing Ed.D (Organizational Leadership).

Website: www.lensoffaith.org
FB: Lensoffaith
Youtube: Lensoffaith
Linked In: Chaundra Gore
Clubhouse: Lensoffaith Speaks
TikTok: Lensoffaithspeaks4

Dr. Paulette Harper is an ordained pastor, a 19-time best-selling and two-time award-winning author, literary strategist, and CEO of Harper Media Global Impact. In recognition of her influence, she has been honored with the 2024 RiseHer Presidential Lifetime Achievement Award and the Passion Purpose Peace Award, presented by Her Excellency Dr. Theresa A. Moseley.

Dr. Harper founded The Reset Conference, to help women renew their minds, refocus their purpose, and realign their lives with God's vision. She also leads BuildHer Kingdom Women Ministries, equipping faith-based women with spiritual and practical tools to build thriving ministries and live out their kingdom purpose.

A resilient survivor of emotional trauma, Dr. Harper has transformed her experiences into a mission to support others. She is a certified Mental Health Coach, holding a Board-Certified Mental Health Coach (BCMHC) credential from the American Association of Christian Counselors. As a distinguished speaker, she empowers individuals to embrace their divine purpose, overcome adversity, and create lives aligned with faith and success.

Through Harper Media Global Impact, Dr. Harper has coached hundreds of first-time authors, guiding them in writing, publishing, and launching best-selling books. Her expertise in self-publishing and literary strategy has made her a trusted mentor for authors seeking to make an impact through storytelling.

Committed to personal and professional excellence, Dr. Harper continues to build platforms that inspire, educate, and empower individuals to lead with purpose and passion. Whether through her books, coaching programs, or conferences, she remains dedicated to helping others achieve breakthroughs in life, leadership, and business.

Connect with Dr. Paulette Harper
Website: www.pauletteharper.com

    Her Excellency Dr. Theresa A. Moseley is a United Nations Peace Ambassador, United States Army Veteran, International Keynote Speaker, 25x-Best Selling Author, a 3x-Award Winning Educator, and a retired educator after 27 years of service. H.E. Dr. Moseley is the owner and Chief Executive Officer of TAM Creating Ambassadors of Peace LLC. Her company provides motivational speeches on passion, purpose and peace, professional development on Transformational Leadership, and seminars on the essential soft skills for effective leadership. Dr. Moseley has an annual live event and a three-day annual virtual Passion Purpose Peace Summit to promote world peace and inner peace.

    Dr. Renyetta Johnson is a wife, mother, devoted follower of Christ and founder of LiveWell 414 LLC, a faith-based Christian counseling and life coaching ministry. She is committed to helping individuals embrace healing and wholeness. Dr. Johnson has authored several impactful works, including Light A Fire: Cultivating, Rekindling, and Experiencing Spiritual Intimacy with a Holy God, The Light A Fire Prayer Journal, and When I Call Him: A 40-Day Prayer Journal for Mothers, all available on Amazon. She is an active contributor and blogger with the EmPowered Purpose Academy as an EmPowered Thought Leader and host of the LiveWell 414 Podcast.

    Connect with Dr. Renyetta Johnson
www.livewell414.com

    LeAnn Cerise Hendrick is the founder and owner of Beyond The Call, Inc, Beyond The Call, LLC and the owner of Sacred Praise Dance Ministry. LeAnn is a best-selling author, a mobile notary, a domestic violence advocate, a motivational speaker, a financial broker, a native Washingtonian, a mother, a grandmother, a mentor, a motivating FORCE and committed servant of the Lord who firmly believes in family, community, and ACTION!

    LeAnn has been awarded numerous humanitarian and community service awards but recently received an Honorary Doctorate of Christian Leadership, the Presidential Lifetime Achievement Award, and Silver Award.

    www.beyondthecalling.com
    Email. lhendrick@beyondthecalling.com

Donna Yates, a Liberty Chaplain and founder of "Voices of Healing," believes in the power of sisterhood and community found in Christ. As a three-time bestselling author, through her writing, Donna's mission is to empower others, reflecting the love and grace she's found in her own journey.

As CEO of Donna Yates and Associates, she guides families in building, protecting, and preserving wealth, understanding that true security comes from faith and wise stewardship. She also champions holistic well-being as a Zinzino Independent Partner. She is a wife, mother, and Yaya to her nine heartbeats.

Connect with Donna Yates
Website: donnayates.com
Donnayates30@gmail.com

Coach Stephanie Johnson is a best-selling author, dynamic keynote speaker, and Certified NLP Practitioner dedicated to empowering individuals through transformative coaching. As a Holistic Health & Wellness, Life, Leadership, and Branding Coach, she helps clients unlock their full potential by bridging the gap between confidence, life, and leadership. With her unique approach, Stephanie Johnson inspires personal and professional breakthroughs, guiding individuals toward clarity, purpose, and success. Her expertise and passion have made her a sought-after mentor for those ready to step into their power and redefine their future. Connect with her to start your transformative journey today.

www.coachstephjohnson.com

Evangelist Krystal Ryan, published author of Through it All Her Story, Empowered by Faith a Devotional for Women, co-author of the best-seller The Unstoppable Black Woman: Sisterhood Edition, and co-author of Focused and Aligned Part 2 Unshakeable Faith, is a native of Newport News, Virginia. A mother and grandmother and the founder of Beyond Blessed Ministries Outreach—an organization birthed from Krystal's personal story of escape and survival of domestic abuse.

Krystal's work has been featured in 5280 Magazine, The Denver Urban Spectrum, and 9 News in Denver, Colorado. She has also been a panelist and guest speaker at several community and ministry events.

Melissa Duran, RN, BC-FMP – Aesthetic & Wellness Spa Owner, Healer, and Faith-Driven Practitioner

Melissa Duran is an aesthetic and wellness spa owner dedicated to healing through faith and medicine. With 28 years in healthcare, including ICU and ER experience, she founded Remedy Spa in Salinas and Carmel to merge science with holistic wellness. Passionate about biohacking, functional medicine, and self-care, Melissa helps clients reduce pain, restore balance, and achieve optimal health. She believes true wellness combines medical expertise with the natural healing tools God provides. She sees Remedy Spa as God's business, stewarding His vision to transform lives through beauty, health, and faith.

Email: melissa@remedyspa.net
Facebook: MelissaDuran

    Minister Regina Amos is a dynamic leader, author of three published works and life coach who empowers women to reach their full potential. With a Psychology degree and certification in Life Coaching, Regina has served in various roles, including Chainbreakers Prison Ministry Lead and Outreach Lead at Greater New Bethel Apostolic Church.

    Professionally, Regina is the Visionary and CEO of BE Life Coaching, where women are encouraged to BE who they were created to BE, unapologetically. Regina also excels as a manager in the nonprofit industry, supporting through program development and execution.

    Regina is the proud mother of three, grandmother of three, she is affectionately called "Gigi".

Coach Renita Crump was called to serve women years before she became a Certified Professional Grief and Loss Coach. She has been trained and certified in grief and loss, anger, depression, and loneliness. She is also a Board-Certified Mental Health Coach, and owner of Visions TLC Coaching and Consulting where she specializes in navigating women through grief, discovering their purpose, and restoring their joy while maintaining wellness in the process. She is also an author and an informative speaker. She is confident, consistent, and committed.

Coach Renita hears your voice, but listens to your heart.

Contact Coach Renita
Email: visionslifecoach1@gmail.com

    Patricia Saulsbury serves as Executive Pastor at Overcomers in Christ Ministries located in Elgin, South Carolina. Known for her maternal wit, wisdom, and infectious prayer life, Pastor Pat has garnered spiritual sons and daughters throughout the country. Her life experience and insight from God's Word has made her a dynamic coach and mentor to young families seeking to balance work, ministry, and family life. As expected, she spends much of her time in devotion and service to the body of Christ and most importantly, to her husband of 45 years, Pastor John Saulsbury, their three children, and four beautiful grandchildren.

    Mother of Zion Judy Wyndham is a powerful woman of God who has been in ministry for over 56 years. She started at Moody Bible Institute and has traveled state to state preaching and teaching the Word of God. She continues as a prophetic watchman for God to pray heaven down and enjoy the manifestation of God's blessings upon her life and her family. She is the mother of Derrick Pearson, who preceded her in death, Al Pearson, and Prophetess Chaundra Gore. She is the grandmother to four granddaughters and three grandsons.

Dr. JoAnne Hayes is a co-author of the best-selling anthologies, My Walk Past Hell and For Such a Time as This. With expertise in business administration, legal acumen, and servant leadership, she leads by example and champions education for all ages.

A graduate of North Carolina A&T State University, Dr. Hayes earned her doctorate from Walden University during the pandemic. A proud member of Zeta Phi Beta Sorority, she advocates for domestic violence survivors and mentors youth in her faith-based community. A dedicated mother, Glam-ma, and community member, she enjoys crafting, sewing, and reading, inspiring others to learn and thrive.

Contact Information:
https://linktr.ee/drjoannehayes

Laticia Cunnigham is an ordained evangelist, author, and certified wellness coach dedicated to helping women overcome trauma through God's grace and mercy. Known as a passionate cheerleader for women, she has spent years inspiring and empowering them to achieve their goals. Her belief is simple yet profound: You can't truly live until you heal—healing is living. Through faith, encouragement, and wisdom, she guides women toward spiritual and emotional restoration.

Connect with Laticia Cunnigham and begin your journey of healing and growth at www.ladiekisha.com.

Christina Aguilar is a mother, wife, caregiver, and entrepreneur with a passion for encouragement. She became an author in 2017, contributing to Breaking Through Barriers Volume 2 and Broken into Brilliance. Her books, including When Queens Rise and Women with Unshakable Faith, are Amazon bestsellers. Christina also launched Unique and Beautiful Boutique, an online jewelry business. As a caregiver, she offers compassion and support, inspiring others through faith. Through her books, testimonies, and motivational speaking, she encourages people to trust God's love, embrace resilience, and walk boldly in their purpose.

Connect with Christina:

Email: aguilar.christina1113@gmail.com
Facebook & Instagram: Christina Aguilar

Best-selling author Isabelle Ramos contributed to Virtuous and Victorious Women: A 30-Day Devotional (June 2025) and the anthologies Women with Unbreakable Faith (April 2023) and Sisters Who Pray (April 2025). A devoted prayer warrior, she enjoys cooking, arts and crafts, and sharing Jesus' love with her grandgirls. Isabelle and her husband, Anthony, have been married for 52 years and divide their time between Northern California and their "second home" in Hawaii. They are blessed with four children, ten grandchildren, and two great-grandchildren.

IG: www.Instagram.com/passion4healthwealth.com
Website: Https://inspired1000.wixsite.com/sisters-who-pray

Sonja Sells, a Business Empowerment Growth Strategist, ignites the fire within women 35+ who are suffocating under rigid schedules and unfulfilling work, empowering them to build passion-fueled online businesses. Through Sonja Sells Enterprises LLC, she offers the Break Free. Be Fierce. Transformation Program, using the T.I.M.E. Framework—Truth, Ignite, Momentum, Empower—to guide women towards financial and lifestyle freedom. Her experience as an Executive Assistant to high-performing entrepreneurs fueled her passion for empowering others. Sonja also founded Chakelet Drap Inspired LLC, a publishing company, and hosts "The Sonja Empowers Show" podcast.

Connect with Sonja Sells
Website: www.SonjaSells.com

In 2024, Cristina achieved a major literary milestone as a contributing author in the bestselling anthology Becoming The Chayil Woman, inspiring others with her story of strength and faith.

Beyond real estate and writing, Cristina has made a meaningful impact as a full-time caregiver, demonstrating compassion and resilience in providing support to her grandfather. Her dedication to helping others extends into the community, where she actively assists the houseless by providing essential resources and sharing the love of Jesus with them.

Connect with Cristina
Email: alanizcristina01@yahoo.com
IG: Alaniz_Cristina_78
Facebook: Cristina Alaniz

Dr. Regina A. Turner is a prophetic life coach, mentor, and visionary dedicated to empowering Kingdom entrepreneurs through Wealth God's Way and God's CEO 365. With a deep prophetic insight and a passion for equipping leaders, she guides women pastors, business owners, and visionaries in aligning their purpose with divine strategies for success through mentorship, training, and prophetic coaching.

Dr. Turner helps leaders navigate their spiritual and business journeys with clarity, confidence, and kingdom authority. Her mission is to activate faith-driven women entrepreneurs to build wealth, influence, and legacy—God's way. Dr. Turner is an overcomer of many trials, but came out a winner.

Connect with Dr. Regina A. Turner @ www.drreginaaturner.com

Prophetess Margaret D Kirk has been an entrepreneur for 25 years, starting in the beauty and wellness industry. She became a licensed esthetician in 2000, earned her bodywork massage license in 2003, and later obtained a B.S. in Organizational Management. In 2016, she acquired two wellness and beauty brands.

She also served on a community board, helping small business owners secure grants and loans. Beyond business, Prophetess Margaret is a licensed Prophetic minister, providing prophetic insight, strategic solutions, and prayer to those in need of spiritual guidance. Her passion lies in empowering others through business, wellness, and faith.

Prophetess Margaret D Kirk, B.S. Ae. LMT Franchise
Dwellness7@gmail.com

Patricia Ann Parada is a devoted evangelist, mentor, and first-time author featured in Virtuous & Victorious: A 30-Day Devotional. With a passion for teaching the Kingdom of God, she mentors men, women, and youth, guiding them in faith and spiritual growth. Patricia is a proud mother of seven beautiful grown children, a loving grandmother to 17 grandchildren, and a blessed great-grandmother. Her heart for ministry and dedication to spreading God's word continue to inspire those around her. She believes in living a life of faith, love, and purpose, empowering others to walk boldly in their divine calling.

Contact Patricia
paradapatty209@gmail.com
Facebook - Patricia Parada

Lashon Dorsey, a lover of the Lord, wife, mother, grandmother, author, speaker, and a Family Nurse Practitioner-BC who serves her community. She is also the owner and founder of E3fit and Wellness LLC, where she pours and builds healthy frameworks into culture and the kingdom of God.

Lashon believes in educating and empowering people to grow to the max level of living on purpose. Her passion is prayer, women, family, community, and kingdom. Lashon is a builder of great men and women, her greatest desire is to equip people for life!

Email- Wellnessfit916@gmail.com

Dr. Jewel White Williams is an educator, wellness advocate, and founder of BlackTie Legacy™, a business dedicated to helping educators and communities prioritize health and well-being. Her journey in health sciences and education has shaped her mission to empower others to care for themselves first, walk in boldness, and create a lasting legacy. Through Dr. Jewel's work—whether speaking, teaching, or leading wellness initiatives—she inspires others to embrace faith, wellness, and purpose. She believes that true impact begins with self-care and intentional living, allowing individuals to thrive spiritually, mentally, and physically as they fulfill their God-given purpose.

Contact Information:

LinkedIn: https://www.linkedin.com/in/jewelwhitewmsdhsc/

Email: support@jwhitewilliams.com

    Anita McAlister is a dedicated educator with over 35 years of experience, passionate about being a positive influence in the lives of children. I also worked as a Certified Nurse Assistant for eight years after completing her college training. Anita founded Spoken Word Ministry to inspire others through uplifting messages and leads Evolution Homeless Ministry, an organization that provides essentials and support to those experiencing homelessness, including helping some find shelter. She also served as a church secretary, assisting with various administrative tasks. In every role, Anita strives to lead with compassion, purpose, and professionalism.

KoJuvona Telfair-Singleton is a Registered Nurse with over 20 years of experience specializing in acute care and long-term care. Throughout her career, she has taught individuals to become Certified Nursing Assistants.

As a nurse manager, KoJuvona dedicated herself to managing the care of our veterans in a veteran's long-term care facility, helping their families transition from home to a nursing care facility.

Now, as Mrs. Singleton takes a sabbatical from nursing, she continues to advocate for geriatric patients, especially for her elderly parents; she also encourages and advises nurses to exemplify empathy and advocating for patients.

Besides nursing, KoJuvona has a passion for helping the broken-hearted and leading them to Jesus Christ.

Email: ktelfair123@gmail.com
Facebook: KoJuvona Telfair-Singleton

Dr. Rhonda A. Bolden is the wife of Archbishop Willie Bolden. She has been speaking and ministering for over 35 years at numerous retreats, conferences, schools, colleges, cCorporate offices, and churches (including The Potter's House – Bishop T.D. Jakes).

She is a best-selling author of 10 books, in which her 4 books and 3 CDs were all released on the same Day. She hosted TV/radio Shows, including TCT Network reaching over 100 million worldwide. She had Covid and cancer, while her husband was on the ventilator 35 days from Covid, but God brought them through GLORY!

Visit: TriumphantWomen.org

Elder Dawn D Braithwaite is the CEO and Founder of B. Encouraged Outreach Ministries, Inc.

She has been ministering the gospel through the word, song, and service to others for over 26 years. She is a podcast host - Thursday Night with Lady Dawn B on the Bravo with Sheila Network via YouTube, holding discussions to help foster and create better relationships of all kinds. She has co-authored 7 book collaborations and is currently working towards obtaining her Doctorate in Biblical Studies.

Connect with Dawn D. Braithwaite:
Ladydawnb19@gmail.com

Candice Bryant is a loving, vibrant, free spirited Berkeley girl, born and raised! She is an Air Force Veteran, retired Registered Nurse, actor and author of the motivational, inspirational life guidebook It's Time. A book guiding people to get unstuck, change their mindset, and live Positive on Purpose.

Candice's gift is encouragement and she uses her gift in her everyday life, pouring love and light into everyone she encounters.

Candice's ultimate goal is to bring people to Christ to live a life full of joy, love, and peace, fulfilling their soul's desires and living life with no regrets.

Candicebryant47@gmail.com

    As a 23-year Army Veteran, transformational life coach, results-driven business consultant, and founder of Aligned Life Leadership & Strategy Group, Dr. LaTonya Poole empowers individuals to build structure, gain clarity, and live with bold, purpose-filled intention. She's also the visionary behind The Eighteen Forever Foundation, a nonprofit committed to ending teen suicide and advancing mental health and wellness through education, advocacy, and compassionate community outreach. Her life's mission is rooted in igniting change—helping others realign their lives with confidence, intention, and resilience. Dr. Poole brings a powerful blend of strategic insight, heart-centered coaching, and lived experience to every client that she serve.

    Connect with Dr. LaTonya Poole
    Website: www.drlatonyapoole.com

    Pastor Sheila P. Ingram, a New York City mother of three, is a multifaceted recording artist and global minister. Her international ministry impacts nations, spanning Barbados , Amsterdam, Africa, and beyond. Author, motivational speaker, and clinical counselor, she leads Women in Pursuit of Purpose. Ingram owns Healthy Taste Buds and Wellness and creates weekly content for two YouTube channels. Her six gospel music projects have positioned her as an opening act for Donnie McClurkin, Helen Baylor, the Clark Sisters, Daryl Coley, and Melba Moore. Pastor Ingram's life powerfully weaves faith, health, and artistic expression, reaching diverse audiences globally.

    Dr. Prophetess Natasha Lawson known as The Vision Doctor, is an international transformational speaker, prolific prophet, and 7x global bestselling author. She is the founder of the Kingdom Purpose Talk Show, Lawson Enterprises, Triumphant Path Ministries, and Emerging Voices Consulting & Solutions.

    Dr. Lawson's 6-Tier Vision Elevation Process, D.O.C.T.O.R, empowers individuals to unlock their potential. A passionate advocate for SDG 17: Partnerships for the Goals, she has been honored as one of the Top 50 Impactful Women and recognized as the 2025 Kingdom Humanitarian Innovator. Dr. Lawson inspires vision-driven change and global collaboration.

    In the Kingdom of God, Prophet Rebecca Huggins is committed to fulfilling her calling by equipping the saints with the word of God as well as serving as one of His prophetic voices confirming esteeming believers with the word so that they are able to live prosperous lives.

    Professionally, Rebecca is a 30-year veteran middle level Instructional Leader who specializes in school transformation, student achievement as well as Curriculum & Instruction. Additionally, she holds numerous degrees and certifications.

    In Marketplace Ministry, Master Coach Rebecca is the President of Leader's Circle University where she assists her partners in creating content and managing their social media platforms, writing their solo and anthology literary works, creating profitable online courses as well as certifying coaches.

    Peshon Allen is a devoted follower of Christ, wife, mother, worship leader, speaker, and bestselling author. An Army Veteran and licensed minister, she founded the podcast and ministry Women In Ministry On The Move!—an empowering online show for women in ministry. She holds degrees in Theology and Communications, is a Presidential Lifetime Achievement Award recipient, and is a proud alumna of American Forces Network. Married to Tyron Allen for 24 years, they share two children. Born in Chicago, Peshon believes in the power of faith, education, and perseverance. Her life motto: "All things are possible with GOD—just believe and trust Him."

    Connect on Facebook@Peshonallen IG: @iampeshon

Write With Us

Be Part of Our Next Divine Collaboration!

We invite you to be part of something extraordinary—The Chayil Woman Experience, an empowering anthology and transformative retreat designed for women ready to embrace their divine strength, wisdom, and purpose.

This next installment in our Divine Collaboration series is more than just a book; it's a movement. Through this anthology, we explore the essence of the Proverbs 31 woman—the Chayil Woman—unveiling her unwavering faith, resilience, and spiritual authority. Your voice, your journey, and your testimony have the power to inspire and uplift others as we bring these timeless virtues to life.

Beyond the pages, The Chayil Woman Experience offers an exclusive retreat—an immersive encounter where luxury meets spiritual renewal. This sacred gathering is designed for women who desire a deeper connection with God, themselves, and a community of like-minded sisters. Prepare to be refreshed, realigned, and empowered through moments of prayer, reflection, and rejuvenation in a setting that nurtures both the soul and the spirit.

Don't miss the opportunity to be part of this divine sisterhood, sharing your story and experiencing a retreat unlike any other.

To learn more about this life-changing experience, visit: https://www.adivinecollaboration.com.

A Divine Collaboration Founders:

Dr. Paulette Harper &

Prophetess Chaundra Gore

Calling All Readers

Join the Movement: Supporting Virtuous & Victorious

We hope that Virtuous & Victorious: A 30-Day Devotional for the Proverbs 31 Woman has inspired, uplifted, and strengthened your faith. Your journey doesn't end here—you have the opportunity to help spread this message and impact even more lives!

If this devotional has blessed you, we invite you to leave a review on Amazon. Your words—no matter how brief—can encourage others to pick up this book and embark on their own transformational journey.

Here's how you can further support this movement:

<u>Recommend It</u> – Share Virtuous & Victorious with your book club, women's ministry, or small group. Your recommendation could be the encouragement someone needs.

<u>Gift a Copy</u> – Instead of passing along your copy, consider purchasing one for a friend, sister, or mentor who would benefit from these powerful devotions.

<u>Share on Social Media</u> – Post your favorite quote, takeaway, or a photo of your book using #VirtuousAndVictorious to help inspire others.

<u>Invite Us to Speak</u> – Whether it's a virtual event, a podcast, a Clubhouse or Facebook Live conversation, or even an in-person gathering, we would love to connect and share more about this divine collaboration.

<u>Host A Divine Collaboration in Your City or State</u> – If you'd love to bring this movement to your community, let's connect! We are passionate about expanding this mission and would love to partner with you.

Your support means the world to us! Together, we can continue uplifting and empowering women to walk boldly in their faith and purpose.

Thank you for being part of this powerful journey!

A Divine Collaboration Founders:

Dr. Paulette Harper &

Prophetess Chaundra Gore

Made in the USA
Middletown, DE
20 June 2025

77175262R00070